KU-134-607

This book is written in simple yet dramatic style, and illustrated in full colour, to bring the story of Jesus vividly to life. The chapters are introduced by a brief historical note, together with the Bible reference from which they were taken.

John Bailey works for the City of Manchester Education Committee as a District Inspector with special responsibility for Moral and Religious Education. He has written and edited many books for children, including *Stories from the Old Testament*, also published by Beaver. He lives with his wife and family in Mellor, near Stockport.

Stories from the
New
Testament

retold by John Bailey

Beaver Books

First published in 1982 by
The Hamlyn Publishing Group Limited
London · New York · Sydney · Toronto
Astronaut House, Feltham, Middlesex, England

© Copyright Text John Bailey 1982
© Copyright Colour Illustrations
Christian Publishing Company Limited 1982
© Copyright Line Drawings
The Hamlyn Publishing Group Limited 1982

ISBN 0 600 20508 8

Printed and bound in Italy
by Graficoop
Set in Baskerville

Contents

1 The Birth of Jesus   7

2 John and the Baptism of Jesus   13

3 The Disciples of Jesus   19

4 Jesus in Galilee   24

5 People Jesus Met   30

6 The Teaching of Jesus   38

7 The Road to Jerusalem   44

8 The Final Conflict   51

9 Trial and Crucifixion   58

10 The Resurrection   66

11 The Gospel of John: 1   73

12 The Gospel of John: 2   79

13 The Early Church   86

14 Paul and the Mission to the Gentiles   93

15 Paul's Second Missionary Journey   101

16 Paul Revisits Asia   109

17 Paul Returns to Jerusalem   115

18 The Shipwreck   122

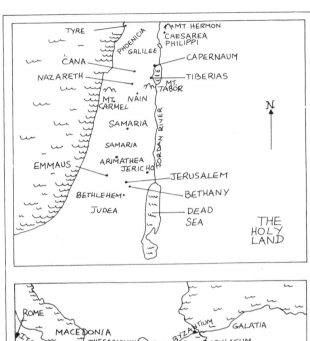

THE HOLY LAND

1 The Birth of Jesus

*The stories of the birth of Jesus contain
two main strands. One traces his ancestry
back through Joseph to King David, and the
other emphasises his special nature through
the miracle of his birth from a virgin
mother. In the sense that it symbolises
the Christian belief that Jesus is the Son
of God, this story could be called a myth.
Many Christians believe it to be literally
true.*

MATTHEW 1,2 LUKE 1,2

Mary, a young girl who lived in Nazareth, near Lake
Galilee, was engaged to Joseph, a skilled carpenter of
the town who could trace his ancestry back to King
David.

One day when Mary was sitting at home, she had a
very strange experience. She went into a trance, and
dreamed that a messenger from God appeared to her.

'Greetings, Mary,' the messenger said. 'The Lord
is with you.'

Mary was very puzzled by this. What could it all
mean?

'Don't worry!' said the messenger, smiling. 'The Lord God has chosen you for a special task. You are to have a son and you must call him Jesus. He is going to be a great man; the people will call him Son of the Most High God. He will be given the throne of David, and will be king of Israel for ever.'

The vision faded away, and Mary was left rubbing her eyes and wondering if it had really happened.

After this, Mary went to stay with her cousin Elizabeth, who lived in a village near Jerusalem. Elizabeth was older than Mary, and had thought that she was past childbearing age. But her husband Zechariah, a priest, had also had a vision in which a messenger of God had told him that Elizabeth would have a baby, who was to be called John. The messenger said that John would be a great man, a second Elijah, who would prepare the way for the Messiah whom the Jews were expecting. Zechariah, he said, would lose the power of speech until the baby was born. Zechariah found this all very difficult to believe.

Elizabeth was delighted to see Mary, and when she heard that Mary was also expecting a baby, she was quite overjoyed. Mary began to tell her all about the dream and the messenger from God, half expecting Elizabeth to laugh at her. But Elizabeth, remembering Zechariah's experience in the temple, was not at all surprised and clapped her hands for joy.

'Mary, you are truly blessed by God,' she said. 'Zechariah has been told that the child I am expecting is to be the forerunner of the Messiah. I believe your son will be that Messiah — the King we have been waiting for ever since the exile.'

Some time later, when Joseph and Mary were married and it was nearly time for Mary's baby to be born, the Roman Emperor Augustus ordered that everyone in the empire should go to their home town to be registered in a census. Joseph came from the village of Bethlehem, near Jerusalem, so even though Mary was pregnant, they had to make the long journey there.

They arrived late at night, and Joseph set about finding somewhere to stay. Of course, many other people were travelling at that time because of the Roman census, and all the rooms were taken. Joseph and Mary had to spend the night in an outhouse at the back of the inn, sharing it with the cattle and donkeys. Later that night, in the squalor and filth of the stable, Mary's baby was born.

Knowing that the baby was due soon, Mary had brought swaddling clothes – bands of cloth that people used at that time – with her to wrap the baby in. When he was securely wrapped up, she laid him gently in a bed of straw in a manger, and she and Joseph settled down to try and get some rest.

Not far away, on the hillside near the village, shepherds were looking after their flocks. They were sitting round a fire, chatting or dozing, when suddenly they were dazzled by a great light in the sky. They were terrified, but a reassuring voice spoke to them and calmed their fears.

'Don't be afraid!' the voice said. 'I bring you good news. A baby has been born in Bethlehem who will be the Messiah, the new David you have all been waiting for. Go into Bethlehem at once, and you will find the baby wrapped in swaddling-clothes, lying in a manger.'

It seemed to the astonished shepherds that they could hear singing: a great chorus of sound, like an angelic choir, singing praises to God. Then the light faded from the sky, and the sound was no more.

Scrambling to their feet, the shepherds left their flocks and ran excitedly into the village. They soon found the stable, and gazed in awe and wonder at the tiny baby, fast asleep in the manger. Some of them fell on their knees and worshipped him. They told their story to everyone who would listen. People were amazed, and thought they were out of their minds, but Mary remembered the words of the messenger from God, smiled to herself, and hugged the baby tightly to her breast.

Some time later, three wise men from the east arrived at the court of King Herod in Jerusalem.

They said they were astrologers; they had seen a new star in the sky, and believed it to be the birth star of a great king. They had brought gifts, and wished to pay homage to the baby.

Herod, not surprisingly, was very put out by this unexpected visit. As a puppet-king of the Romans, he felt very insecure at the best of times; a rumour of a baby born to be king of Israel was the last thing he wanted. He called the chief priests and lawyers together, and asked them where they expected the Messiah to be born.

'At Bethlehem, in Judah,' they replied, quoting from the book of the prophet Micah.

Herod thought for a while, then he called the wise men to him. He smiled insincerely at them.

'My advisers tell me that the child will have been born in Bethlehem,' he said. 'Please be so good as to seek out the child. When you have found him, let me know, so that I may also pay homage to him.' Naturally, Herod's real intentions were quite different.

He gave the strangers directions to Bethlehem, and they set off at once. When night fell, the star again appeared, and the wise men were delighted to see that it was directly above the village they were heading for. They went into the house where Mary and Joseph were living, knelt down in homage before the child, and offered him expensive presents – gold, frankincense and myrrh. Then they stabled their horses and camels and retired to the inn for the night, well pleased with the success of their journey.

That night, the three men had a vivid dream, in which they realised that Herod really intended not to worship Jesus but to kill him. When they got up next morning, they did not return to Jerusalem but went home another way.

After they had gone, Joseph was also warned in a dream that Herod would try to kill the child, and he decided that the safest thing for them would be to leave the country for a while. So taking Mary and Jesus on a donkey, Joseph went to Egypt, where they stayed until the news came through that Herod was dead. Then Joseph knew that it was safe to return to Israel, and they made their way back to their home in Nazareth.

2 John and the Baptism of Jesus

*John the Baptist was the last of the Old
Testament prophets, calling people to
repentance and proclaiming the Messiah
who was to follow him. Jesus saw in John
the spirit of Elijah, preparing people for his
own ministry – see Malachi chapter 4,
verse 5.*

*Prince Herod, who arrested John,
was the son of King Herod. He was the
Tetrarch of Galilee, and is also called
Herod Antipas.*

MARK 1,6   MATTHEW 3,4,11,14   LUKE 3,4,7

Elizabeth, Zacharias's wife, gave birth to a son, just
as the messenger of God had told Zechariah in his
vision. They called the boy John, and he grew up to
be a spokesman for God like the prophets of old. He
lived alone in the Judaean hills, and when God called
him to be a prophet, he went round the whole
country telling people to give up their wrong-doing
and turn again to God.

When Mark came to write about John the Baptist
many years later, he found a passage in the writings of
the prophet Malachi which he decided fitted John
exactly:

'Look, before the day of the Lord comes God will
send the prophet Elijah to you.'

Mark decided that John must have been Elijah
reborn, to prepare the way for Jesus.

Luke also searched the Old Testament writings,
and he thought that John was the one that the
prophet Isaiah wrote of during the time of the exile in
Babylon:

A lonely voice crying in the wilderness,
    'Prepare the way for the Lord,

Clear the path ahead of him.
Every valley shall be filled
And the mountains and hills levelled,
The sharp corners rounded off
And the rocky tracks made smooth;
And everyone shall see the power of God
Working to save mankind.'

John used to dip people in the waters of the River Jordan as a sign that their sins were washed away. This is called baptism, and he became known as John the Baptist. Many people used to come out to the Jordan to be baptised by him, and to listen to his preaching, for which he was famous.

'You sons of snakes! Who warned you to escape from the punishment to come?' he would say to them. 'If you're really sorry for your evil ways, then prove it by living better lives. It's no good saying "We are the children of Abraham". I tell you, if God wanted to he could make children of Abraham out of these stones lying about.'

His followers began to wonder whether John was the Messiah, the new king they had been expecting for so long. John soon put a stop to that idea.

'O yes, I baptise you with water,' he said. 'But the one coming after me is far greater than I am. I'm not fit to fasten his sandals. He will baptise you with fire; he'll sort out the wheat from the chaff, and throw the chaff on to a fire that never goes out.'

One day, when Jesus was thirty years old, he came out to the wilderness by the River Jordan to see John, his cousin. He asked John to baptise him too, but John refused.

'I am the one that ought to be baptised by you,' he said. 'And yet you have come to me!'

'I think it is what God wants,' Jesus said gently.

So John baptised Jesus in the River Jordan. As Jesus came out of the water, he had a vision of the skies opening and God's spirit coming down to him, like a dove. Then he heard a voice:

'This is my dear son, who pleases me very much.'

Jesus knew then that he really was called by God for some special purpose. He decided to go off on his own into the desert, to try and think out what it all meant. He spent many days alone in the rocky desert hills, sometimes finding water but going without food, and he grew very hungry. As he sat one day in the hot sun, the stones and boulders of the desert shimmering in the heat looked to him like loaves of bread.

'If I really am a son of God, I could turn these stones into bread,' he thought to himself.

Then he shook himself, and dismissed the thought. Food isn't that important, he told himself; certainly not important enough for God to interfere with the laws of nature.

Later on, Jesus found himself on the edge of a rocky cliff, looking down at the steep drop below. He was reminded of the steep wall on the south-east corner of the temple mount in Jerusalem, with the drop down to the Kidron valley below it.

'I could jump off,' he thought. 'I wouldn't come to any harm; God would send his angels to catch me. That would prove to everyone that I really was someone special!'

When he thought more about it, however, Jesus dismissed this temptation too. If God wanted to terrify men into obeying him by showing them supernatural tricks, obviously he could do so at any time. But God wanted men to turn to him of their own free will.

Then Jesus went up to the top of the highest mountain in the area. He could see as far as the Mediterranean to the west, the great snowy peak of

Mount Hermon to the north, and the rocky desert of Arabia to the south and east.

'The people are expecting a king, a Messiah,' he thought. 'Someone to drive out the Romans. I could be that king, and then I would rule over all this land as far as the eye can see.'

On reflection, however, Jesus came to see that this wasn't what the Messiah was meant to be. God wasn't interested in earthly kingdoms; God's kingdom was in the hearts of men. Somehow, he would have to show people what the kingdom of God really meant.

Still deep in thought, Jesus made his way back to where he had last seen his cousin John. On the way, however, he heard that John had been arrested by Prince Herod. Jesus at once made up his mind. He would go back to Galilee, and start preaching the good news of the kingdom of God.

Mark tells us that the reason Herod arrested John was that John had told Herod he had no right to divorce his wife and marry Herodias, his brother's wife. Herod kept John in prison, but did not dare to put him to death because he was so popular. Herod's wife Herodias, however, was determined that John should die. Her opportunity came on Herod's birthday. Herod gave a great banquet for all the top people in his province, Galilee. When they all had had plenty to drink, Herodias dressed her daughter Salome in a revealing costume and sent her in to dance for them. She was a great success, and when the applause died down, Herod called her over.

'Lovely, lovely,' he said. 'You danced beautifully, my dear. You shall be rewarded. Anything – ask for anything you like.'

Salome could see that Herod was more than a little drunk, so she went over to her mother for advice.

'Ask for the head of John the Baptist on a meat-plate,' Herodias hissed.

Startled, Salome went back to Prince Herod.

'You said I could have anything I liked,' she said. 'I would like you to give me the head of John the Baptist on a dish.'

Herod was trapped. He had made a promise which everyone had heard, so he had to keep it. Reluctantly, he gave the order, and his soldiers executed

John in his prison cell. They brought his head into the banqueting hall, and Salome had to accept the gruesome object, which she gave to her mother.

When the disciples of John heard about his death, they came and collected his body and gave it a decent burial.

3 The Disciples of Jesus

*The message Jesus preached, and his
striking personality, provoked different
responses; hostility and opposition from those
who felt threatened, and devoted loyalty
from his followers – the disciples.*

MATTHEW 4,9,10,12,16,20   LUKE 5,8,9,12
MARK 2,3,6,8,10

The disciples, or followers of Jesus, were ordinary
working men: fishermen, a customs-officer, a member of the resistance movement. None of them were
priests, or members of the official religious groups
such as the Pharisees or Sadducees. The disciples
were not even very good at obeying the religious laws
of the time; on the sabbath, when they were hungry,
they plucked corn and ate it, which was against the
strict Jewish law. And they weren't especially strong
or brave; although they had given up everything to
follow Jesus, they all fell asleep when he needed them
to stay awake and pray with him in the Garden of
Gethsemane, and when he was arrested they all ran
away.

The first disciples were two brothers from Bethsaida, Simon and Andrew. They were fishing in the
lake of Gennesaret (or Galilee) when Jesus called
them. Jesus may, of course, have known them for
some time; he had been living in Nazareth for thirty
years. Or perhaps they had heard him preach; Luke
says Jesus started telling the good news of the
kingdom in the synagogues round about before he
called any of his disciples. Anyway, when Jesus asked
them to leave their nets and go with him, Simon and
Andrew had no second thoughts but went at once. A
little further along the beach, Jesus came across two
more brothers, James and John, the sons of Zebedee.

19

They were also fishermen. Again, when Jesus called them they left everything – their father, their boat, their nets – and followed him.

Next day they left Bethsaida to go to the district of Galilee, on the west side of the lake. On the way they met Philip, who also came from Bethsaida. Jesus called Philip to join them. He, too, came without hesitation, stopping only to call for his friend Nathanael.

'Nathanael, you must come at once!' he cried as he ran towards him. 'We have found the Messiah, the leader we've been waiting for. It's Jesus, the son of Joseph of Nazareth!'

Nathanael was, however, harder to convince. 'Can any good thing come out of Nazareth?' he replied.

Nevertheless, he went along with Philip. When Jesus saw him coming he said to the others, 'Here is a true Israelite; there is nothing deceitful about him.' Nathanael was astonished at the way Jesus could see what he was like at first glance, and he too became a disciple.

Jesus and his disciples went about Galilee for some time, preaching and healing the sick. One day they passed a customs-house, and Jesus noticed a customs-officer called Matthew sitting counting the takings. 'Matthew, come with me!' Jesus called to him. Matthew got up at once, left the money he was counting, walked past his astonished fellow-officers, and became a disciple of Jesus.

Jesus eventually picked out twelve disciples to go out and preach the Gospel. They were called the apostles, which means 'sent out'. Jesus gave them authority to preach and to heal, and sent them out to proclaim the good news of the kingdom of God. He warned the twelve that following him would not be easy. He told them they would be arrested, flogged, even killed; everyone would hate them. But they were to have confidence; when they were called upon to speak of what they believed, the spirit of God would speak through them. Even families would be divided – some for Jesus, some against him. Once, when Jesus was speaking to a crowd of people, his mother and brothers came to see him. They couldn't get through the crowds, so someone brought a message to Jesus to tell him they were there.

'Who is my mother? Who are my brothers?' Jesus

asked the messenger. He turned to the crowd, and pointed to his disciples.

'These are my family now,' he said. 'Anyone who obeys the will of my heavenly Father is my mother, my sister or my brother.' (Jesus said this to show how important the disciples were to him. It did not mean that he had ceased to love his own family. When, later, he was crucified, he was thinking of his mother just before he died, and entrusted her to the care of his close friend and disciple, John.)

Jesus told people who were thinking of following him that they must care more for him than for their own families. 'No one is worthy of me who does not take up his cross and follow me,' he said. But he also promised that his followers would be given strength by God. 'The yoke I will give you is easy to carry, and the load I will give you is light.'

One of the twelve disciples was Simon, whom Jesus renamed Peter – 'the rock'. One day when Jesus was praying and talking with the twelve, he asked them who they thought he was. Peter was the one to put into words what they were all thinking. 'You are the Messiah,' he said.

Jesus gave them strict instructions not to tell anyone, because he knew people would misunderstand. He began to explain to them that the Son of Man (the name Jesus used to describe himself) must suffer and die.

'Heaven forbid, Lord!' exclaimed Peter. 'This will never happen to you!' Jesus looked at him sadly. Peter, so quick to say what was in his mind, had a long way to go before he would understand Jesus.

After some time in Galilee, Jesus decided it was time to go to Jerusalem. To get there they had to pass through the country known as Samaria, and the Jews and the Samaritans hated each other. On the journey, Jesus sent messengers ahead to a village in Samaria to ask for lodgings for the night, but they were turned away. John and James, when they saw this, were furious.

'Master, may we call down fire from heaven to burn this village up?' they demanded. They, too, did not understand how Jesus intended to use his power. They were such a hot-tempered pair that Jesus called them the Sons of Thunder. Their mother, Zebedee's wife, was very ambitious for them, but she too could not understand that the kingdom Jesus was talking about was not an earthly kingdom. One day she came to Jesus to ask a favour.

'Master,' she said, 'grant that when you come into your kingdom, my two sons John and James may sit either side of you, one on your right and one on your left.'

Jesus sighed, and tried to explain to her and to John and James that his path was one of suffering, not of glory.

When the other ten heard about this, they were very indignant with John and James, and began to argue among themselves about who was the greatest. Jesus tried again to explain to them all.

'The Son of Man did not come to be served, but to serve others,' he said to them.

But this was a lesson which was too hard for the disciples to understand, and it was not until after his death and resurrection that they began to see that the kingdom he had spoken of was not an earthly kingdom, but the rule of God in men's hearts.

4 Jesus in Galilee

On the face of it, Galilee was an unlikely place for Jesus to begin his ministry. Why not Jerusalem, the centre of Jewish worship? Galilee was a foreign province, which had been repopulated by Jews only a hundred years or so before. But the people of the northern part of Israel had always maintained that they had kept more closely to the traditions of the covenant with God than the southern kingdom of Judah.
Jesus made Capernaum, the fishing village on the shores of the Sea of Galilee, his base during this part of his ministry.

MATTHEW 8,9   MARK 1,2,6   LUKE 4,5

After he had returned to Galilee and called the disciples, Jesus started preaching the good news that the kingdom of God had begun. Like John the Baptist before him, he called people to admit that they had been doing wrong things, and to turn again to God. He spoke with an air of quiet authority which forced people to sit up and take notice. He went with his

disciples to the synagogue in Capernaum, and preached to the people there, causing quite a stir.

'He's not like the usual rabbi, is he?' they said. 'This one sounds so sure of himself. Perhaps he really has brought a message from God.'

There was a man in the congregation at Capernaum who was mentally ill; people there believed that a devil or demon had taken over his mind. When this man saw Jesus, he went into a frenzy.

'What do you want with us, Jesus of Nazareth?' he shrieked. 'Have you come to destroy us?'

Jesus, knowing that they all believed the man was possessed by a demon, spoke directly to the demon.

'Be quiet, and come out of him,' he said.

The man had a kind of fit, foaming at the mouth and thrashing his arms and legs about. Then he gave a loud cry and sat up, rubbing his eyes. He looked around, puzzled.

'Where am I?' he said.

They told him what had happened, and from then on he was completely normal.

The people of Capernaum were awed and impressed by this display of Jesus' power.

'He speaks with such authority that even demons obey him!' they exclaimed. The news spread rapidly, and before long Jesus was being talked about all over Galilee.

Jesus and the disciples left the synagogue and went to Simon and Andrew's house. When they arrived, they found that Simon's mother-in-law was in bed, suffering from a fever.

Jesus went up to her and sat by the bed. She was moaning and tossing about, delirious with fever. Jesus took hold of her hand, and it seemed as if some strange power flowed from him. She woke up with the fever completely gone, and insisted on getting up straight away and preparing a meal for them.

By the evening, news of Jesus' healing powers had spread through the whole town. When the Sabbath ended at sunset, it seemed that every sick person in Capernaum was outside the door. Jesus went out to them and spoke to each one. His personality seemed to radiate power; many were cured as soon as he spoke to them, and they all experienced some kind of relief or reassurance.

When they had all gone, Jesus was exhausted. He collapsed into bed and fell straight to sleep.

Next morning, when the disciples got up, Jesus was nowhere to be found. Worried, they searched high and low for him. At last they found him, alone in the hills behind Capernaum, deep in prayer.

Jesus opened his eyes and smiled at them.

'I'm sorry,' he said. 'Were you worried about me? I got up early and came out here to be alone with my Father. I had to find out if I was doing what he wanted.'

'We're not the only ones looking for you,' Simon replied. 'After what you did last night, the whole town wants you! There are relatives who want to thank you, people who were cured and want to shake you by the hand – they're all trying to find you.'

Jesus sighed.

'I was afraid of that,' he said. 'That's just what I didn't want. Never mind; let's go on to another town. I must preach the good news everywhere; that's what I came back here for.'

Jesus and his disciples went to all the towns and villages in the region, preaching the good news of the kingdom of God and healing the sick. One day as they were walking along, a leper came up and knelt in front of Jesus.

'Master, I have heard of your healing power,' the

man said. 'I believe you could cure me.'

Leprosy is a very unpleasant disease which in those days was so contagious that lepers were thrown out of their homes and forced to live alone away from towns and villages. People would bring them food and drink, but otherwise they were quite cut off.

Jesus felt sorry for the man and stretched out his hand to touch him. His disciples were horrified, but did not try to stop him.

'Yes, I can heal you,' he said. 'Look – you are whole again.'

The leper looked down at himself, and to his joy and relief, all the symptoms of leprosy had gone. The feeling came back into his hands and feet, and he was cured.

'Go and show yourself to the priest, and make the thank-offering laid down in the laws of Moses,' Jesus said. 'Then you will be able to return home. But don't tell anyone how you were cured.'

The man went off at once, but he spread the story of how Jesus had cured him wherever he went. So everyone wanted to see Jesus. He couldn't go into a town or village without great crowds forming. He and his disciples began to stay out in the countryside, but even so, large numbers of people came out looking for him.

After a few days Jesus went back to Capernaum. The news soon got round that he was at home, and people came from all over to see him and listen to what he had to say. As many as could squashed into the house to listen to Jesus, and the rest waited outside, trying to see what was going on.

Then four men arrived carrying their friend on a stretcher. He was paralysed, and they had brought him to Jesus to be cured. There was no way they could get into the house, so they pushed their way to the staircase on the outside wall of the house and carefully carried the stretcher up to the flat roof. They broke through the roof, and lowered the stretcher down with ropes until the paralysed man was lying in front of Jesus.

Jesus looked down at the man, and somehow sensed that what was really wrong with him was in his mind. He had done something of which he felt so ashamed and guilty that he had become paralysed.

Jesus was deeply impressed by the faith of this man and the determination of his four friends. He smiled at him.

'Don't worry,' he said. 'Those things you can't bear to think about, those awful sins – they are forgiven.'

Some of the lawyers and Pharisees were in the house, and heard Jesus say this. They began to mutter furiously to each other.

'He can't say things like that,' they said. 'That's blasphemy! Only God can forgive sins.'

Jesus heard what they were saying.

'You don't believe that I have the authority to forgive sins, do you?' he said to them. 'Look – I'll prove to you that his sins really are forgiven.'

Jesus turned to the paralysed man.

'You can get up now,' he said. 'Go on – pick up your bed. You can go home.'

At once, the man who had been paralysed got up, picked up the stretcher, and pushed his way past the astonished onlookers.

When Jesus came to his home town of Nazareth, he went to the synagogue on the sabbath as usual. He was invited to read the lesson, and the attendant gave him the scroll containing the writings of the prophet Isaiah and his followers. Jesus opened the scroll at a passage written just after the return from exile in Babylon:

The spirit of the Lord is with me, because he has anointed me. He sent me to bring good news to the poor. To announce that prisoners could go free and the blind regain their sight. To bring relief to the oppressed, and to say that the time has come when the Lord will save his people.

When he had read this out, Jesus rolled up the scroll and handed it back to the attendant. There was dead silence in the synagogue. Everyone was looking at Jesus to see what he would say.

He looked round at the congregation – men who had known him all his life, ever since he was a boy in Joseph's workshop.

'Today, the reading you have just heard has come true,' Jesus said.

There was a stir of resentment.

'Who does he think he is?' said one.

'Isn't he the son of Joseph, the carpenter?' said another. 'How can he be the anointed one of God?'

Jesus was taken aback by their disbelief.

'A prophet is honoured everywhere except in his own home town,' he said sadly.

5 People Jesus Met

*The campaign in Galilee continued among
growing controversy. The ordinary people
were quick to follow Jesus in the hope of
seeing a mircle, but slow to understand
his teaching about the kingdom of God.
And the experts in Jewish law, the Scribes
and the Pharisees, were growing ever more
critical of Jesus because of his freedom
with the sabbath laws and his claim to
direct authority from God.*

MARK 3-5 MATTHEW 8,9 LUKE 8

The meeting of religious leaders, Pharisees and
teachers of the laws of Moses, was not going well.
More and more reports were coming in about a man
called Jesus, who was attracting great crowds
wherever he went in the region of Galilee.

'Apparently he's cured a few simple-minded folk,
and now everyone follows him round in the hope of
seeing a miracle,' said one of the Pharisees.

'Oh, it's much worse than that,' said another. 'He
claims to be able to drive out demons, and says he
does it in the name of God.'

The pious Pharisees shuddered. This was very
dangerous indeed.

'And you should see some of the people he goes
around with!' said another. 'One of his disciples is
that traitor Matthew, who collects taxes for the
Romans.'

One of the scribes, an expert on the law, cleared his
throat.

'I'm afraid you're all missing the point,' he said.
'Many people are able to cast out demons. What
makes Jesus so dangerous is that he claims to be above
the law.'

He consulted his notes.

'Two weeks ago, his disciples were accused of taking corn from a cornfield on the sabbath, in direct disobedience of the sabbath laws. We tackled Jesus about it, and do you know what he said?'

There was a buzz of interest.

'He said, "The sabbath was made for man, not man for the sabbath. The Son of Man is Lord over the sabbath." He's saying that the law of Moses, the whole basis of our religion, doesn't matter any more!'

The others were furious at this. The Pharisees had done a lot to reform the religion of the Jews, and their reforms were based on the importance of the law. They all agreed that from then on, they would watch this man Jesus very closely.

The following sabbath, there was a man in the synagogue who had a deformed arm. The Pharisees and lawyers were very interested to see what Jesus would do.

Jesus saw the man with the deformed arm, and called him out to the front. Then he turned to the Pharisees and the lawyers.

'You are all experts at interpreting the law of

Moses,' he said. 'Does it say one should do good on the sabbath, or evil? Should I save someone's life on the sabbath if I see the need, or should I ignore him?'

They had no reply to this.

Jesus shook his head sadly, and turned back to the man he had called out.

'Stretch out your arm,' he said.

The man did so, and his arm was healed.

When they left the synagogue, the Pharisees began to plot with supporters of Prince Herod, the executor of John the Baptist, to find a way of getting rid of Jesus.

Jesus stayed in Galilee teaching people about the kingdom of God, and healing people who were sick in body or mind. He tried to explain the kingdom to them in pictures or parables. One story was about a man who sowed some seeds on his land, then went away and left it. While he was away, the seed carried on growing, all by itself, without him doing anything. It produced a blade, then an ear of corn, and finally it was ready for harvesting.

This story showed his hearers that the kingdom of God was already among them. God had been at work sowing the seed in men's hearts; now it was ready to come out into the open.

After he had told this story, Jesus wanted to get away from the crowds to rest, so he suggested to his disciples that they should cross over to the other side of the Sea of Galilee in one of their fishing boats. Jesus was so tired that he fell asleep on a cushion in the stern of the boat. A sudden storm sprang up, and waves began to break over the sides of the boat, threatening to swamp it.

The disciples began to panic, and woke Jesus up.

'Master, we are sinking!' they cried. 'Can't you do something? Don't you care?'

Jesus stood up and faced into the wind.

'Be still!' he cried.

At once the wind and waves died down, and the lake became dead calm.

Jesus turned to the disciples.

'Where is your faith?' he said sternly. 'Don't you realise God has work for us to do? He wouldn't let anything happen to us.'

The disciples were very much afraid at this display of power.

'Who is he?' they said to one another. 'Even the wind and waves do what he says!'

They came to the other side of the lake, near the

town of Gerasa, which in those days was not Jewish territory. Just outside the town was an old graveyard, where a madman had made his home. The people had tried to control him by tying him up with ropes and even with chains, but he was so strong he always got away, and so they left him alone. He used to wander about all day among the gravestones, shouting and screaming nonsense.

When he saw Jesus, he went frantic. The disciples, who believed he was demon-possessed, said afterwards that it was as if the demons recognised Jesus.

'What is your name?' asked Jesus quietly.

'Many! My name is Many!' cried the madman. 'There are lots of us!' And he gave a wild cackle of laughter.

Then he stopped and looked shrewdly at Jesus.

'You've come for us, haven't you?' he said. 'I know who you are! Leave us alone!'

'Come out of him, I order you,' said Jesus.

On the hillside next to the cemetery was a large herd of pigs. When the madman heard this command, he clapped his hands over his ears and rushed at the pigs, screaming at the top of his voice.

Squealing and grunting, the pigs stampeded in front of him. They came to the water's edge and

rushed straight on into the lake, where many of them drowned. The madman ran into the water after them, but the shock of the cold water seemed to bring him to his senses, and he stopped and came slowly back to Jesus.

The men who were supposed to be looking after the pigs were terrified. They ran off into the town, and before long a steady stream of townsfolk from Gerasa was coming out to the cemetery to see what had happened.

They found Jesus sitting talking quietly to the man who had been mad. He was by then dressed normally in clean clothes which the disciples had given him, and he was quite recovered.

The people of Gerasa did not know what to make of it. They were very much afraid of this stranger, who could cure madmen and who had apparently caused them to lose a herd of pigs. They conferred together, and then very politely but firmly asked Jesus to leave at once.

When they came back to the Jewish side of the lake, Jesus and the disciples were met by a great crowd of people. While they were still on the lakeside, a man called Jairus came running up to Jesus. Jairus was the president of the local synagogue.

'Master!' he gasped. 'I beg you, come quickly – my daughter – she's dying.'

Jesus went with him at once, with the crowd pressing at his heels. There was a woman in the crowd who suffered from bleeding which would not stop. She had been like this for twelve years, and the doctors could do nothing for her. She managed to get close to Jesus, and reached out and touched him. At once the bleeding stopped and she was cured.

Jesus felt her touch, and somehow knew that healing power had been drawn from him. He turned round to the crowd.

'Who touched me?' he asked.

His disciples wondered what was the matter with Jesus.

'With all these people pushing along behind you, you ask who touched you?' they said.

But the woman who had been cured came forward, trembling with fright, and knelt down in front of Jesus. She had not known what would happen, she had just reached out to Jesus without thinking. She was in a state of shock, and told Jesus the whole story.

Jesus helped her to her feet.

'It was your faith that cured you,' he said. 'Go in peace.'

While he was speaking, a messenger came from the president's house.

'Your daughter is dead,' he said to Jairus. 'There is no need to trouble the rabbi any further.'

Jesus overheard the message, and turned to Jairus.

'Don't give up hope,' he said. 'Have faith in God.'

He went on, allowing only his closest disciples to go with him. When they came to the president's house, they found the whole household weeping and wailing in grief.

Jesus pushed his way through the mourners and went to where the girl was lying. He looked closely at her, then turned to her relatives.

'Don't cry any more,' he said. 'She's not dead; she's in a coma.'

The grieving family were astonished, and their first reaction was to laugh in disbelief. But Jesus turned to the little girl, and took hold of her hand.

'Wake up, my dear,' he said to her. 'It's time to get up.'

Almost as if she were sleep-walking, the girl got up and walked across the room. Jesus told them to give her something to eat, and to let her rest and recover.

6 The Teaching of Jesus

*In order to understand the teaching of
Jesus, one has to try to get back to the time
when Jesus was travelling around teaching
and healing. Most of his teaching was in
the form of parables – stories with a
single, central point – about the kingdom of
God. The point of the story is more important
than the detail.*

The parable of the sower MATTHEW 13   MARK 4
LUKE 8.
The parable of the lost sheep MATTHEW 18
LUKE 15
The parable of the two sons MATTHEW 21
The parable of the good Samaritan LUKE 10

Jesus was a marvellous teacher, and he usually
taught by means of simple stories about the everyday
things and people he could see around him – farmers
and fishermen, sheep and shepherds, rich men, poor
men, fathers and sons. Here is one of his stories.

'One day a farmer was sowing seed for corn,
scattering the seed to left and right as he went. Some
of the seed fell on a footpath, where the ground was

beaten hard; it wasn't there long before the birds came and gobbled it up. Some seed fell on rocky ground, where there was only a thin layer of topsoil; it germinated quickly, but because it had no real roots it withered away in the sun. Some of the seed fell among weeds, which choked it. But some of the seed fell on good soil; it grew strong and tall in the sunshine and yielded a good crop.'

This is one of several parables of the kingdom which Jesus told. Most of his hearers would have seen the point of the story at once, but when Mark came to write it down many years later, he felt it was necessary to add a detailed explanation. He suggested that the seed on the footpath was like people who ignore Jesus; his words just bounce off them. The seed which fell on rocky ground was like people who accepted Jesus's words at first, but gave up when things became difficult. The seed which fell among weeds was like people whose response to Jesus was distracted by things like money and possessions. The seed which fell on good ground stood for people who accepted the words of Jesus and grew into the kingdom of God.

The stories Jesus told, especially the parables of the

kingdom, usually made one simple point that even a child could understand. People often brought children to Jesus and he would welcome them and talk to them; he told his followers that the kingdom of Heaven belonged to people who could become as trusting as little children.

The religious people of the time often used to grumble about the way Jesus mixed with people they regarded as sinners: drop-outs, drunkards, prostitutes and the like. Jesus answered them with this story:

'If a shepherd has a hundred sheep and finds one of them is missing, what does he do? Why, he leaves the ninety-nine in a field and goes off to look for the missing one. And how pleased he is when he finds it! He lifts it onto his shoulders and carries it home, calling out to his friends and neighbours to celebrate with him – he has found his missing sheep. In just the same way, there is more joy in heaven over one sinner who repents than over ninety-nine righteous people who don't need to repent.'

Here is another story Jesus told to make the same point:

'Once there was a wealthy man who had two sons. The younger son came to him and said, "I can't wait

until you die to get my inheritance. Give me my share of the property now."

'His father was very sad at these words, but he worked out what the son's share of the property would be and gave it to him in cash. The younger son took it and went off to another country, where he began throwing his money around wildly. He gambled, he drank, he went to parties; and of course, as long as his money lasted he had plenty of friends. Before long, though, his money ran out, and his so-called friends suddenly disappeared. He tried to borrow, but no one would help him. Worst of all, there was a terrible famine in that country, and he began to starve. He went along to a local farmer to ask for a job, and was set to work looking after pigs.'

At this point his listeners shuddered with disgust. Pigs were regarded by the Jews as unclean animals; they were not allowed to eat them or touch them, and to look after pigs was the most degrading job they could imagine. Jesus continued the story.

'There he was, nearly starving, sitting among the pigs. He was so hungry he was ready to eat the pigswill. Suddenly he came to his senses.

'"What am I doing here?" he asked himself. "My father's paid servants have more than enough food, and here am I, his son, starving to death! I will go home and tell my father how wrong I was, and what a fool I've been. Perhaps he'll take me back as a servant or a farm-labourer. I'm sure he'll not let me starve."

'He left the pig farm there and then, and made his way painfully back to his own country. As he came up the road to his father's house, his father saw him coming. He recognised his son at once, dirty and dishevelled though he was, and his heart went out to him. He ran to meet him, threw his arms round him and kissed him. The son began the speech he had prepared in his mind on the long walk home.

'"Father, I have done wrong, I know. I'm not fit to be called your son . . ." But his father wouldn't let him finish. He sent one servant for a new robe, another for shoes, and another to prepare a great feast.

'The elder brother heard the noise and came in to see what was going on. When he found out that his good-for-nothing brother had come home at last, and his father, instead of throwing him out on his ear, was throwing a party for him, he was furious.

'"All these years I've worked for you," he snarled at his father. "You never gave a party for me – but this layabout turns up, and you get out the red carpet."

'"My son," said his father gently. "You are always with me; everything I have is yours. But your brother . . . he was lost to us, and now he is found. How could we help celebrating?"'

The Jewish authorities and lawyers often tried to test Jesus by asking him awkward questions. Once, a teacher of the Jewish law came up and tried to trap Jesus.

'Rabbi,' he said, 'do you believe in life after death? If so, how can I have eternal life?'

Jesus could see it was a trick question, because the Jews at this time often used to argue about life after death. He turned the question back on the lawyer. 'What do the laws of Moses say? How do you, a lawyer, interpret them?' he asked.

The lawyer thought for a moment, and then quoted a summary of the Ten Commandments: 'Love the Lord your God with all your heart, with all your soul, with all your strength, and with all your mind; and love your neighbour as much as you love yourself.'

'Quite right,' replied Jesus. 'Do that, and you will live.'

The lawyer didn't give up so easily, though.

'That's all very well, rabbi,' he said, 'but who is my neighbour?'

'There was once a man who had to go from Jerusalem to Jericho,' Jesus replied. 'On the way, he was attacked by robbers, beaten up, and left half dead. A priest came by, saw him lying there, and hurried by on the other side of the road. A little while later, a temple servant came by, stopped and looked at the man, and then hurried on. Then a Samaritan, a foreigner, came by. He took pity on the poor man, gave him first-aid, put him on his own donkey, and took him to an inn. He paid the innkeeper to look after the man until he had recovered, and offered to pay any more expenses when he next passed by.'

Jesus paused and looked at the lawyer. 'In your opinion,' he asked, 'which of the three acted most like a neighbour to the man in need?'

'The one who helped him, I suppose,' replied the lawyer.

'Yes, indeed,' replied Jesus. 'Not the priest, not the temple servant, but the foreigner. Go and try to be like him.'

7 The Road to Jerusalem

*Whether the feeding of the five thousand
happened literally as described in the gospels
is perhaps not so important as the richer
meaning which the evangelists draw from it:
the link with the Last Supper. The conflict
with the temptations, where Jesus refused
to turn stones into bread, is more apparent
than real; Jesus does not use the miracle
to compel people to obey.*

*Peter's confession at Caesarea Philippi is
the climax of the first half of the gospel story.
From then on, the teaching of Jesus was
addressed mainly to his disciples, to try
and help them to understand his role as the
Messiah in terms of the suffering servant
of Isaiah.*

MARK 6,8-10 MATTHEW 14,16,17 LUKE 9

When the disciples came back after Jesus had sent
them out in pairs teaching and healing, they were
very tired. Jesus decided that they needed some time
to rest, away from the crowds. They went by boat
across the lake to find a lonely spot well away from
any towns or villages.

Unfortunately, lots of people saw them leave and
guessed where they were going. They hurried off
round the shore of the lake, gathering other people on
the way. By the time Jesus and his disciples arrived in
their boat, the shore was crowded with people eagerly
waiting for them.

'Oh, no!' groaned the disciples. 'There goes our
day of peace and quiet!'

'Shall we carry on round the lake, master?' asked
one. 'They might give up and go home.'

'No, we can't do that,' Jesus replied. 'Look at them

– they're like sheep without a shepherd. I must go and speak to them.'

They beached the boat, and Jesus began to speak to the crowds. The day wore on, but nobody showed any sign of wanting to go home.

In the afternoon the disciples came to Jesus.

'It's getting very late, master,' they said. 'Don't you think we ought to send these people off to get themselves something to eat and drink?'

Jesus was thinking about the talks he was having with the people, not about food.

'Yes, yes,' he said. 'You organise it.'

'You mean we have to buy food for all these thousands of people?' the disciples protested.

'How much food do you have?' Jesus asked.

The disciples went to have a look.

'We have five loaves of bread, and we caught two fish in the lake this morning,' they said.

'Ask the people to sit down on the grass,' Jesus said.

Everyone sat down and Jesus took the bread and the fish and said the blessing. Then he gave the food to his disciples to give out to the people. There must have been five thousand people there, but somehow, despite the small amount of food, suddenly everyone seemed to have something to eat.

Many years later, when the gospel writers came to record what they remembered or what the disciples told them about the life of Jesus, they thought about this story and realised that it was a fulfilment of something Jesus said later, at the Last Supper in Jerusalem. Then, he took a loaf of bread, broke it, and gave it to his disciples, telling them they should do the same, in his memory. This simple action became the central part of the Christian act of worship called the communion, or the mass. The feeding of the five thousand people in Galilee was, in a way, the first communion service.

After this, Jesus and the disciples went north to the town of Caesarea Philippi, on the southern slopes of Mount Hermon.

'Tell me,' Jesus said to them as they were walking along, 'who do people say that I am?'

'Some say you are John the Baptist,' they replied. 'Others think you are Elijah, or another of the prophets come back again.'

'And what about you?' asked Jesus. 'Who do you think I am?'

Peter was the one to reply. 'I think that you

are the Messiah,' he said.

'You are right,' Jesus replied. 'But for the time being, we must keep it secret. So far, nobody really understands what I have tried to teach them about the kingdom of God.'

Jesus began to teach the disciples that the Messiah would not be a great king like David who would drive out the Romans and establish a kingdom in the land of Israel. Instead, the Messiah would be someone who would suffer at the hands of the chief priests, Pharisees and lawyers, just like the suffering servant in the prophecies of Isaiah.

Peter could not believe this, especially when Jesus told them that he thought the authorities would probably have him put to death.

'Master, that will never happen to you!' he said violently.

Jesus looked at him sadly.

'Do you think I am not tempted to try and avoid it, Peter?' he asked. 'I don't want to die, any more than you do. But I believe it is God's will.'

A few days later, Jesus went with his closest disciples, Peter, James and John, up to Mount

Hermon. While they were there, the three disciples suddenly had a vision in which they saw Jesus as a

shining heavenly figure. Two other figures appeared with a bright light surrounding them, and Peter guessed that they were Moses and Elijah.

'Master,' Peter said. 'It is good that we are here with you. Shall we build shelters for you and Moses and Elijah?' He didn't really know what he was saying, they were all so terrified by the experience. Perhaps seeing Moses made him think of shelters, because the Jews had a festival of shelters or booths to remind them of the time when Moses led them through the wilderness.

Then a cloud came over the mountain, and they heard a voice which seemed to come out of the cloud: 'This is my son; listen to him.'

When the disciples looked round, there was no one else there; they were alone with Jesus.

On their way down the mountain, the disciples asked Jesus about their experience. He explained to them that it meant that he was the Messiah, the one chosen by God.

'But we have always been taught that before the Messiah comes, Elijah will come again,' they said.

'Elijah has already come,' Jesus replied. 'John the Baptist was Elijah, and he has suffered and died at the hands of God's enemies.'

When they got back to the other disciples, they found them surrounded by an excited crowd.

'What's all the fuss about?' Jesus asked. A man in the crowd came forward.

'Master, I brought my son to you,' he said. 'He is an epileptic, and has fits and convulsions. I asked your disciples to cure him, but they couldn't.'

'Bring the boy to me,' Jesus said.

They fetched him, and as soon as he saw Jesus he went into an epileptic fit, rolling about and foaming at the mouth.

'How long has he been like this?' Jesus said.

'All his life,' the man replied. 'If it is possible, take pity on us and cure him.'

'If it is possible!' exclaimed Jesus. 'Everything's possible, if you have faith.'

'Master, I have faith!' the boy's father cried. 'Help me where my faith has failed!'

Jesus took the boy's hand and ordered the illness to leave him. The boy had one final spasm, then lay still. Jesus lifted him to his feet and he opened his eyes and was quite normal again.

'He will be all right from now on,' he told the boy's father.

The disciples asked him why they had not been able to cure the boy.

'Some illnesses can be cured easily, if people have faith in you,' Jesus replied. 'Others are more difficult. You must pray and have faith in God yourselves.'

After this, Jesus decided that the time had come for them to go to Jerusalem. The disciples were very much afraid, knowing how much opposition there

was to Jesus among the religious authorities. Going to Jerusalem seemed like walking into the lions' den.

Jesus took the twelve on one side, and tried to explain to them what was going to happen.

'We have to go to Jerusalem to face the opposition,' he said. 'I believe that God wants me to try and show the leaders of Israel a better way. If they won't listen to me, then I must still be faithful to God, even if I have to die. But that will not be the end; God will not desert you.'

His disciples could not understand this, and it was only afterwards that they came to see that he must have been talking about the Resurrection.

8 The Final Conflict

The Evangelists devote nearly one third of their gospels to the events in Jerusalem in the last week in the life of Jesus.

The entry into Jerusalem is a conscious fulfilment by Jesus of Zechariah chapter 9, and was meant to challenge the city to see him as the true Messiah. But the reception given to him by the crowds was the usual one given to pilgrims coming up to the festival of Passover; the people chanted the words of Psalm 118 verse 26, but nobody noticed the symbolic action of Jesus.

The temple markets were controlled by the family of Annas, the high priest, and provided a legitimate service in selling animals for sacrifice. Jesus quotes from Jeremiah chapter 7, verse 11, and Isaiah chapter 56, verse 7, and condemns the materialism of this practice. In challenging the temple authorities, Jesus is deliberately fulfilling Malachi chapter 3, verse 1: 'The Lord whom you seek will suddenly come to his temple.'

The betrayal by Judas Iscariot is probably part of the same deliberate policy of announcing his Messianic claims. Judas betrayed not only the secret meeting place but also the 'Messianic secret', which throughout his earlier ministry Jesus had refused to allow to be be told. The time had come.

MATTHEW 21,22,26   MARK 11,12
LUKE 19,20,22

Jesus and the disciples reached the village of Bethany

on the Mount of Olives, close to Jerusalem. It was just before the great Festival of Passover, and the roads near Jerusalem were thronged with pilgrims going up to the city to celebrate the festival.

Jesus stopped at a house in Bethany where he had friends, and sent two of his disciples on to the next village.

'When you get to the village,' he told them, 'you'll find a donkey tethered to the fence. It's a young donkey, which has never been ridden. Unhitch it, and bring it back here. If anyone asks you what you're doing, just say, "The master needs it – we'll bring it back tomorrow. It'll be all right – it's all arranged."'

The disciples went straight away, and found the young donkey tied up outside a house in the main street of the village, just as Jesus had said. They untied it and started leading it off down the street.

'Hey! where do you think you're going?' a voice cried out suddenly. It was the owner of the house, standing in the doorway.

'The master needs it,' they replied, as Jesus had told them.

'The master, eh?' the man replied. 'I guess that's all right, then. Mind you bring the donkey back, though.'

They went back to Bethany with the donkey, and Jesus came out to meet them.

'Ah, good, you've found it,' he said. 'I'm going to ride into Jerusalem so that everyone knows who I am. Come on, get ready.'

The disciples spread their cloaks on the donkey's back, and Jesus sat on the makeshift saddle. With the disciples leading the way, Jesus rode into Jerusalem. The road was crowded with pilgrims, and all along the way people were throwing down brushwood cut

from the fields, and branches of palm trees. They were greeting all the pilgrims with verses from the Psalms: 'Blessed are those who come in the name of the Lord; blessings on the kingdom of David.'

No one took any notice of Jesus in particular; as far as the people of Jerusalem were concerned, he was just another pilgrim who had come up for the festival. Little did they know that they were greeting the man who in himself brought the new kingdom of David.

Disappointed, Jesus dismounted from the donkey, and handed the reins to one of his disciples.

'That's it, I'm afraid,' he said. 'Nobody wants to know us today. Take the donkey back, and I'll think of another way to show them who I am.'

They went back to Bethany for the night, and returned to Jerusalem the next day. This time, they went straight to the temple. The Court of the Gentiles was crowded with pilgrims, buying lambs, goats and pigeons for sacrifice. They had to pay in special temple money, and there were money-changers everywhere, changing Greek or Roman money into the special Jewish coins.

Jesus stood with the disciples taking in the scene: the noise, the bustle, the greed, the profit. How can anyone possibly worship here, he thought?

'Listen to me!' he cried out. 'Have you not read in the prophet Isaiah, "My house shall be called a house of prayer for all nations?" Does this look to you like a house of prayer? You have turned it into a robber's cave!'

He strode over to the tables of the money-changers and began turning them over, scattering money in all directions. The people took their cue from him, and cheering wildly, drove the money changers and the animal salesmen out of the temple. Then Jesus began to teach the people about the coming of the kingdom of God, just as he had done in Galilee.

The chief priests and lawyers met hurriedly as soon as they heard about the incident. They wanted to get rid of Jesus before he did them any more damage, but they did not dare move against him openly because his teaching was so popular.

Next day, the chief priests and lawyers went up to Jesus where he was teaching the people.

'What right have you to teach these people?' they said. 'Who gave you authority to come here and do these things?'

Jesus looked at them steadily.

'I have a question for you, first,' he said. 'If you can

answer me, I'll tell you by whose authority I am here. The baptism of John – was it from God, or not?'

The chief priests and lawyers conferred hastily among themselves.

'If we say John was from God, he'll say why don't we accept him too?' said one.

'Yes, and if we say John was not from God, the people will stone us,' said another. They decided to compromise.

'We are not yet in a position to give you the official answer to that question,' they said to Jesus. 'The matter is still being investigated.'

'Then I am afraid I am not yet in a position to give you the official answer to your question,' Jesus said to them. The crowd roared with laughter, and the chief priests and lawyers went away embarrassed and humiliated.

The Pharisees and the supporters of Herod also tried to trap Jesus.

'Master, we know you are honest, and teach honestly the law of God,' they said. 'Tell us: are we right in paying taxes to the Roman emperor? Is that God's will?'

Jesus could see that they were trying to catch him out. If he said it was wrong to pay the Roman taxes, he would be in trouble with the authorities, but if he said it was right, every patriotic Jew would be against him.

'Fetch me a silver piece, and let me look at it,' he said.

They brought a Roman coin and handed it to him.

'Whose head is it on this coin, and whose inscription?' Jesus asked.

'Caesar's,' they replied.

'Then give to Caesar that which is Caesar's, and give to God the loyalty due to God,' Jesus said.

Once again, his opponents retired defeated. But they continued to look for an opportunity to seize him when he was not surrounded by people.

The time came for the Passover meal, when the Jewish people celebrated their escape from Egypt thanks to the angel of the Lord passing over their houses but killing the first-born Egyptians. Jesus sent two of his disciples into the city.

'When you go through the city gate,' he said to them, 'a man will meet you carrying a jar of water. Follow him, and when he goes into a house, go in with him. Ask the owner of the house to show you the room reserved for the master to eat the Passover meal with his disciples. Then get everything ready for the meal.'

The disciples did as Jesus said. Meanwhile, Judas Iscariot, one of the disciples, was getting tired of waiting for Jesus to act. He was convinced that Jesus was the man to lead a revolution against the Romans, and he decided to force his hand. He went to the chief priests, and told them who he was.

'This Jesus claims to be the Messiah,' he said. 'If you will make it worth my while, I'll show you where you can arrest him - tonight, in a quiet spot well away from the crowds. You'll have no trouble.'

They agreed on the sum of thirty pieces of silver, and Judas went away well satisfied. Now, if Jesus was the Messiah, he would be forced to take action when the chief priests came to arrest him. He would use all his powers, Judas thought, and the revolution would begin. The scene was set for the final showdown.

9   Trial and Crucifixion

The various accounts of the Last Supper in the New Testament show Jesus presiding over a meal which was at once a precursor of the eternal banquet in the kingdom of God, and also a memorial of his own forthcoming death on the cross.

The hastily-convened trial before the Sanhedrin does not appear to have been conducted according to the strict rabbinic regulations, and may have been a private examination rather than a trial. In reply to the high priest's direct question, Jesus quotes Psalm 110, verse 1, and Daniel 7, verse 13. The Jewish authorities did not have the power to exact the death penalty, and Jesus had to be taken before the Roman authorities. The accusation before Pilate, that Jesus claimed to be the 'king of the Jews', forced the Roman governor to take action.

Crucifixion was a form of execution used widely by the Romans. The condemned man had to carry the cross-bar to the place of execution. It was normally a lingering death, and both Pilate and the centurion were surprised that Jesus died so soon. The loud cry uttered by Jesus is a cry of triumph. The psalm which he quoted, Psalm 22, 'My God, my God, why have you forsaken me', goes on to become a psalm of praise: 'Let all the ends of the earth remember and turn again to the Lord, let all the families of the nations bow down before him.'

MARK 14,15   MATTHEW 26,27   LUKE 22,23

58

That evening, Jesus sat at table with the twelve in the room which had been prepared for the Passover meal.

'You know,' Jesus said, 'one of you is going to betray me. Someone who is eating with us now.'

They were all very upset at this, and began to press Jesus to say whom he meant.

'Surely you don't mean me?' each one said. But Jesus would not tell them.

'I will only say this: I am following the path laid down for me by God, but I am sorry for the man who betrays me. It would have been better for him never to have been born.'

During the Passover supper, Jesus took the bread, said the blessing, and solemnly broke it.

'Take this, and eat it,' he said to them. 'It is to remind you of me, and of my body, which will be broken for your sakes.'

Then he took the cup of wine.

'Share this between you,' he said. 'It is the blood of the new agreement with God, and it is shed for all people. I shall not drink wine again until I drink it new in the kingdom of Heaven.'

Then, singing the Passover hymn, Jesus and the

disciples went out towards the Mount of Olives. Jesus was very quiet, and Peter asked him what was the matter.

'I was remembering that passage in the prophet Zechariah,' Jesus said. 'You know, where he says: "The shepherd will be struck down, and the sheep will be scattered." I think it means that when I am arrested, you will all deny ever knowing me.'

'The others may disown you, but I never will,' Peter declared hotly.

Jesus looked at him sadly.

'Before cockcrow tomorrow, you will have denied me three times, Peter,' he said.

When they came to a garden known as Gethsemane, Jesus asked the disciples to wait for him while he spent some time in prayer. He was suddenly overcome by a feeling of sheer terror at the thought of having to face death alone.

'Wait here for a while, and stay awake with me,' he said to the three. Then he prayed desperately to God.

'Show me another way, Father, so that I don't have to die,' he prayed. 'But if there is no other way, I will do what you want.'

He went back and found Peter, James and John asleep.

'Could you not stay awake with me for one hour, Peter?' he said. 'Wake up, and pray that you don't have to face a real test of your strength.'

Just then there was a great clattering of armour and weapons, and Judas appeared at the head of a column of temple police and soldiers. Judas went straight up to Jesus and kissed him on the cheek. This was the signal he had agreed with the chief priests. At once, the guard seized Jesus, and held him fast.

It all happened so quickly, the sleepy disciples had no time to do anything. One of them pulled out his sword and struck out at a servant of the high priest, cutting off his ear. But Jesus ordered him to put away his sword.

'What do you take me for? A bandit?' he said to the temple police scornfully. 'You could have arrested me at any time, when I was preaching openly in the temple.'

They led Jesus away, and his disciples fled in terror. Among them was a young man who had followed them to the garden in the hope of hearing Jesus teach. This young man later became a friend of Peter, and wrote the first gospel; his name was Mark.

Jesus was taken to the high priest's house, where all the chief priests, lawyers and elders had gathered. Peter followed at a safe distance, and waited outside the courtyard by the fire.

A great many witnesses were brought against Jesus, but they couldn't agree among themselves and the chief priests could find no real evidence to justify the death penalty. The high priest decided to question Jesus himself.

'What have you to say in reply to these charges?' he asked. Jesus would not reply.

'Do you, or do you not claim to be the Messiah?'
the high priest shouted angrily.

Jesus looked at him steadily.

'The words are yours,' he said. 'But I tell you this:
you will see a son of man sitting on the right hand of
God, and coming on the clouds of heaven.'

The high priest turned to the council.

'Do you need any further witnesses?' he asked.
'You have all heard this man's blasphemy. What is
your verdict?'

The decision was unanimous: Jesus was guilty, and
should be put to death.

Meanwhile, Peter was still waiting in the courtyard. A serving maid came up and looked at him
curiously.

'Weren't you one of the followers of Jesus?' she
asked.

'I don't know what you're talking about,' Peter
said. He went out to the porch, but the serving maid
began pointing him out to the men in the yard, saying
he was one of the men who had been with Jesus.
Again Peter denied it.

One of the men came over to Peter.

'I reckon you are a follower of Jesus, you know,' he

said. 'Your Galilean accent gives you away.'

Peter cursed, and swore that he didn't even know Jesus. Then he heard the cock crow, and remembered what Jesus had said. He ran out, weeping bitterly.

Next morning, the chief priests took Jesus in chains before Pilate, the Roman governor.

'This man claims to be king of the Jews,' they said. 'We demand the death penalty. If you won't execute him, you are no friend of Caesar.'

Pilate had Jesus brought before him.

'Is this true?' he asked.

'The words are theirs,' Jesus replied. And to Pilate's surprise, Jesus would not say any more.

Pilate knew that the chief priests and religious leaders were trying to force his hand, and he looked for a loophole in the law. Every year, at the Passover festival, the Governor used to release one prisoner to the crowd. Pilate went out on the balcony, and spoke to the pilgrims in the square.

'Shall I release Jesus, the king of the Jews?' he asked them.

The chief priests had planted men among the crowd, and they began to shout for Barabbas to be set free instead. Barabbas was a Jewish nationalist who had been arrested by the Romans for rebellion.

The crowd took up the cry. 'Barabbas! We want Barabbas!' they yelled.

Pilate was taken aback.

'What shall I do with this man Jesus?' he asked.

'Crucify him!' a voice cried out.

'Yes, yes, crucify him! Crucify!' the crowd roared.

Pilate had not the courage to stand against a mob. Meekly he signed the death penalty, and Jesus was led away to be executed, while Barabbas was released.

The soldiers first took Jesus down to the courtyard,

and began to mock him. They dressed him in a purple robe like a king, forced a rough crown of thorns on his head, and pretended to salute him.

'Hail, king of the Jews!' they jeered, beating him and spitting on him. Then they put the cross-bar over his shoulders, and led him away to the place of execution.

When Jesus stumbled under the weight of the heavy cross-bar, the soldiers forced a bystander, a man called Simon from Cyrene, to carry it for him.

They came to the hill called Golgotha, which means 'the place of the skull'. Jesus was offered drugged wine, but he refused it. Then he was nailed to the cross, and the cross was hoisted upright. The soldiers divided his clothes among themselves by throwing dice. They wrote down the charge against him and put it on the cross: 'THE KING OF THE JEWS'. Two criminals were crucified at the same time, one either side of Jesus.

The crowd mocked and jeered at Jesus as he hung helpless on the cross, his body racked with pain.

'He saved others, but can't save himself!' they cried. 'If you really are the Messiah, come down from the cross – then we'll believe you!'

At midday, it suddenly went very dark. The crowd fell silent and began looking round uneasily. The darkness lasted for three hours, and the victims of the crucifixion weakened visibly. The only sound was the rasping of breath in their lungs as they painfully pushed themselves upwards to be able to breathe, then slumped down again with their weight taken on their arms.

Suddenly, Jesus cried out: 'My God, my God, why have you forsaken me?'

Some of the onlookers thought he was calling for Elijah. One of them soaked a sponge in wine and held it up to Jesus on a long cane, but Jesus turned his head away. Then Jesus gave a loud cry, his head fell forward, and he died.

10 The Resurrection

*The accounts of the empty tomb in the
four gospels are impossible to harmonise.
All we can be sure of is that the tomb was
found empty on the Sunday morning, and that
on various occasions Jesus appeared to
many of his followers, in both Galilee
and Judaea.*

*The resurrection appearances are recorded
to teach the Church of Christ that Jesus was
spiritually present among them. Luke
concludes the ministry of Jesus with an
account of his ascension into heaven.*

MARK 15,16 MATTHEW 27,28 LUKE 24
ACTS OF THE APOSTLES 1

Not all of the Jewish leaders in Jerusalem had been
opposed to Jesus. One respected member of the
council, Joseph of Arimathaea, had been very
interested in what Jesus had been saying about the
kingdom of God. Joseph had been against the policy
of the chief priests and religious leaders who had
wanted Jesus arrested, but he had been outvoted.

When Jesus was taken to be crucified, Joseph stood
with the crowd watching the scene. He felt sickened
by the mocking and the insults that they hurled at
Jesus, but there was nothing he could do to stop it. He
watched as Jesus was nailed to the cross, and waited
with the disciples until Jesus died.

Then Joseph made up his mind. He had not been
able to prevent the death of Jesus, but at least he
could make sure that he was given a decent burial. He
hurried away to Pilate, the Roman governor, and
asked permission to take the body of Jesus for burial.

Pilate was surprised to hear that Jesus was dead

already; sometimes the victims of crucifixion lingered for two or three days. He made no objection, and Joseph hastily went back to Golgotha, taking with him his friend, Nicodemus, who had also been a secret admirer of Jesus.

They took down the body from the cross, and wrapped it in a linen sheet. They had to hurry, because it was now getting quite late on the Friday afternoon and the sabbath began at sunset on Friday.

Joseph had had a tomb cut out of the rock in a garden quite near by, which he had intended for his own burial. He and Nicodemus now carried the body of Jesus to this tomb, laid it inside and anointed it with a mixture of myrrh and aloes which Nicodemus had brought with him. Then they covered the body with the linen sheet, rolled a large rock over the entrance to the tomb as a protection against thieves and wild animals, and hurried back into Jerusalem for the sabbath.

Some of the women who had come with the disciples from Galilee and had been present at the crucifixion had followed Joseph and Nicodemus to see where they put the body. They wanted to prepare the body for burial, not knowing that Nicodemus had

already brought spices for the same purpose. They took careful note of the tomb where the body of Jesus had been placed, meaning to return as soon as the sabbath was over.

That sabbath was a long and difficult day for the disciples. They dared not go out of the house for fear of being arrested, and they were racked with guilt and fear. Everything they had been working for and looking forward to seemed to have been lost. For Peter, it was even worse. He had sworn to stand by Jesus, and at the first challenge, he had denied even knowing him.

It was worst of all, however, for Judas. He had betrayed Jesus, confident that Jesus would be forced to use his great powers and start the revolution against the Romans. And now Jesus was dead. It was more than Judas could bear. He took a rope, and went out and hanged himself.

Early on the Sunday morning, as soon as the sabbath was over, the women went out to the tomb, carrying spices to anoint the body of Jesus for burial. When they came to the garden, they found to their astonishment that the stone which had blocked the

entrance to the tomb had been rolled away.

Anxiously, they went inside. The linen sheet was lying there, but otherwise the tomb was empty.

Terrified, the women ran out of the tomb. Then something happened that stopped them and held them riveted. Afterwards, they could not agree on what exactly they had seen; one said a young man, one said an angel, one said two men in shining white robes. As they stood there, the vision spoke.

'Do not be afraid,' he said. 'You are looking for Jesus of Nazareth, who was crucified. He is not here; he is alive. Go and tell the disciples that he has gone ahead to Galilee, and they will see him there.'

Overjoyed and hardly able to believe it, the women ran back to the house where the disciples were staying, to tell them the news. But the disciples thought the women were hysterical; they didn't believe them.

Later that day, two of the disciples were walking to Emmaus, a village seven miles (about eleven kilometres) outside Jerusalem where they had friends. On the way, another traveller joined them and asked them why they were so gloomy. They looked at him in surprise.

'You must be the only person staying in Jerusalem who doesn't know what's happened in the past few days,' they said.

'What do you mean?' the man asked.

'Why, about Jesus of Nazareth, of course,' one of the disciples replied. 'You must have heard of him – the prophet from Galilee? We had all been hoping that he was going to be the Messiah. But the chief priests and the council arrested him and handed him over to Pilate, to be put to death. He was crucified last Friday.'

'And that's not all,' the other disciple added. 'This morning, some of the women in our group went to the tomb to get his body ready for burial, and found the tomb empty. They came back with some extraordinary tale about seeing angels, who told them that Jesus was still alive.'

'Some of the men ran to the tomb to check,' the first disciple said. 'The tomb was empty, just as the women had said. But they didn't see any angels.'

To their surprise, the traveller began to quote passages from the scriptures, to show that the Messiah had to suffer and die before he could begin his rule. The disciples listened eagerly, remembering things

Jesus had said to them before his death which they had not understood at the time.

In no time they found themselves at Emmaus. The stranger was going to continue on his journey, but the disciples urged him to stay for a while.

'It's nearly night-time,' they said. 'Why don't you stay with us, and have a meal?'

They sat down at table, and the stranger took the bread and said the blessing over it. Then he broke it, and gave it to the disciples. Suddenly they knew it was Jesus. As the realisation dawned on them, the stranger disappeared and they found themselves alone.

'I thought there was something familiar about him, as we were walking along the road!' one of them exclaimed.

'This can only mean the women were right!' the other disciple said. 'We must go back to Jerusalem and tell the others!'

Even though it was nearly dark, they left at once. They went straight to the house in Jerusalem where the rest of the eleven were staying, and burst in excitedly.

'It's true!' they said, panting.

'We've seen him! He really is alive!'

The other disciples crowded round, wanting to know more.

'Where did you see him?' they demanded. 'What did he look like? What did he say?'

The two disciples did their best to answer all the questions. They explained that they hadn't recognised him at first, but when he had broken the bread they had suddenly seen that he was Jesus.

While they were all talking about it, suddenly Jesus was there in the room with them. They fell silent; it was like seeing a ghost.

'Why are you so afraid?' Jesus asked. 'Don't you believe the evidence of your own eyes? It really is me, not a ghost. Touch me, and see for yourselves. No ghost has flesh and bones like I have!'

They could still hardly believe it, because it seemed too good to be true.

'Have you anything to eat?' Jesus asked.

They offered him some fish which the women had just cooked, and Jesus took it and ate it as if nothing had happened.

'Do you understand now, what I told you about the Son of Man having to suffer and die?' he asked. 'You are my witnesses. I want you to wait here in Jerusalem until God's Holy Spirit comes to you. Then you are to go out and tell the whole world what has happened here in Jerusalem.'

Then, as they watched, he seemed to vanish from sight, and they knew he had gone to be with God.

11 The Gospel of John: 1

*This gospel is taken separately because its
style is so different from the other three.
It is covered in this story and in Story 12.
It was written later than the synoptic gospels,
probably about AD 100, and there is a
tradition that the author was John the son
of Zebedee, beloved disciple of Jesus.*

*John takes the traditional elements of the
life of Jesus and handles them freely,
altering the order in the light of his overall
understanding of the significance of Jesus.
The gospel has a very formal structure.
It begins with a philosophical prologue,
followed by the story of John the Baptist.
Then the public ministry is recorded in
sections, each beginning with a 'sign' and
followed by a long, theological discourse.
Next there is a long, private discourse
between Jesus and his Father, and finally
there is the account of the Passion.*

*This selection from the fourth gospel
consists largely of incidents not recorded
in the synoptic gospels, and simplified excerpts
from the discourses.*

JOHN 1,2,4,5

John, the disciple of Jesus, was by this time an old
man. He lived quietly in Ephesus, looked after by a
loyal group of friends who had been converted to
Christianity many years before, when the apostle
Paul had first visited Ephesus. Many times his friends
had urged John to write down what he remembered
about Jesus, and those months when Jesus had been
teaching and healing in Galilee and Jerusalem.

John smiled at the memories. He often told his friends that Jesus was, to him, like a word spoken by God: part of God, and yet separate; showing men something of what God wanted them to be like, and yet leaving them to listen or not, as they chose. John wondered how he could possibly explain to his friends just how big a change Jesus had made in his life. He told them a story to try to make it clear to them.

'Once upon a time, Jesus went to a wedding with his disciples. Everything went smoothly until, half-way through the wedding feast, the wine ran out. Jesus's mother, who had also been invited, came up to Jesus and asked him if he could do anything about it. He didn't want to help at first, I could tell. He said something about not being ready. But his mother wouldn't take no for an answer, and Jesus ordered the servants to fill up six stone water-jars with water.

They couldn't see any point in that, and Mary had to speak quite sharply to them to make them do what Jesus asked. Anyway, they went off grumbling and filled the jars, and then Jesus told them to draw some off and take it to the master of ceremonies. He tasted it, and declared it was better than the wine they had served up at first. This is the first clue that I'm going to give you about Jesus.'

His friends puzzled for a long time about the meaning of this story. Had Jesus really turned water into wine? None of the other gospel-writers, Mark, Matthew or Luke, had said anything about it. What did John mean? He wouldn't tell them; just smiled that dreamy, faraway smile of his, and left them to sort it out for themselves. Some of them thought it meant that Jesus was like a rich, new wine, compared with the thin, useless water of the old Jewish laws. But they couldn't all agree, and Christians are still wondering about it today.

Another story John told them was about a time when Jesus and the disciples were travelling through Samaria, which lay between Galilee and Judaea. The Jews had been at loggerheads with the Samaritans for centuries.

'We came to a spring, which they call Jacob's Well,' John said. 'Jesus sat down, and some of the disciples went off into the nearby village to buy food. While we were waiting, a Samaritan woman came up to draw water from the well. Jesus asked her for a drink, and she was very surprised that he should even speak to her. "What, you, a Jew, want a drink from

me, a Samaritan?" she said. "If you knew who I am," Jesus replied, "you would have asked me and I would have given you living water." The woman didn't know what he meant. She looked confused, and said something about Jesus not having a bucket. "When you drink this water, you are soon thirsty again," Jesus said. "I will give you the water of life. Anyone who drinks that will never be thirsty again."

'The woman was very impressed and realised that Jesus was a prophet. She asked him who was right, the Samaritans who worshipped God on Mount Gerizim, or the Jews who worshipped in Jerusalem. Jesus explained to her that true worship comes from the heart, not from any particular place. Then the woman guessed that Jesus was the Messiah.'

One of the questions which worried the early Church was whether the good news of the kingdom was meant for all mankind, or only for the Jews. Paul had paved the way by baptising non-Jews, and eventually the leader of the early Church, Peter, had accepted this as God's will. John's Christian companions at Ephesus were all non-Jews, and they often used to talk about Paul and his arguments with Peter. John told them a story to show them that Jesus had always intended the kingdom to be for Jews and non-Jews alike.

'We were visiting Cana in Galilee, where Jesus had turned the water into wine,' he said. 'We met an officer in Herod's government, a foreigner, whose son was lying dangerously ill at his home in Capernaum. He came up to Jesus and begged him to go along with him to Capernaum and heal the boy. Jesus wouldn't go at first; he was tired of people wanting proof. "None of you will believe, will you, unless you see miracles and wonders," he said. "Sir, I believe in you," the officer said. "Please come, before my boy dies." Jesus saw that he really did have faith. "Go home," he said. "Your boy will live." The man believed him and left for Capernaum at once. On his way home, his servants met him with the news that his son had recovered. "When did it happen?" he asked. They told him, and it was the exact time that Jesus had said that the boy would live. That's the second clue I'll give you about Jesus.'

John's friends found it hard to understand why the Jews had wanted to kill Jesus. If he went about doing good and healing people, surely they couldn't have objected to that? John told them the following story to explain how Jesus had upset the lawyers and Pharisees.

'On one occasion, Jesus went up to Jerusalem for one of the Jewish festivals. Near the sheep pool there is a place called Bethesda, where blind, lame and paralysed people wait in the hope of being healed in the waters. Jesus was walking past Bethesda when he saw a crippled man lying there. Jesus asked him if he was hoping to be cured, and the crippled man said he had no one to lift him into the water. Jesus took pity on him, and told him to get up, pick up his bed and walk. He did so, and found to his amazement that he was cured.

'Now, all this took place on a sabbath. When the Jewish leaders saw the man carrying his bed, they wanted to know why he was breaking the sabbath laws. "The man who cured me told me to carry my bed," he said to them. The Jews realised that it was Jesus who had cured the man, and they went to look for Jesus to ask him what he meant by it.

'"My Father has never stopped working, and neither do I," Jesus told them.

'The Jews became very angry at this. Not only was Jesus breaking the sabbath, he was also claiming equality with God. Now do you see why the Jews wanted to kill him?'

12 The Gospel of John: 2

JOHN 6,8,9,11,13,20   EPHESIANS 1

The Christians in Ephesus who looked after John in his old age often used to ask him about things that puzzled them in the gospels of Mark and Luke. One story which they found very difficult was the Feeding of the Five Thousand. Did it really happen, they asked John? Did the five loaves and two fish really turn into enough food for five thousand people?

'I'll tell you something that Jesus said, and then you might understand,' John replied. 'The people were following him everywhere, and wouldn't give him any rest. "Are you just following me in the hope of seeing a miracle?" Jesus asked them. "If so, you've got your values all wrong. The bread I gave you to eat won't last; you should be looking for spiritual food."

'"Do you mean bread from heaven, like the manna that our ancestors were given in the wilderness?" they asked.

'"I am not talking about the food which you eat," Jesus replied. "I am speaking of real bread from heaven, which gives men a new kind of life."

'"How do we get this bread from heaven?" they asked.

'"I am the bread of life," Jesus told them. "Anyone who comes to me will never be hungry. I came from heaven to bring new life to all who have faith in me."

'The Jews could not understand this. "Surely this is Joseph's son?" they said. "We know his father and mother. How can he have come down from heaven?"

'But you should be able to see exactly what Jesus meant. You share in the breaking of bread every Sunday, and you should find in that fellowship the new quality of life that Jesus promised.'

The Ephesians were satisfied by this answer, and

realised that in many of the stories about Jesus it was more important to look for the deeper meaning than to ask whether or not it actually happened.

One day, some of John's friends were reading through a copy of a letter from the Apostle Paul.

'What does Paul mean,' they asked John, 'when he says that he prays that our inward eyes may be opened, so that we may know what it is we are called to? What are our inward eyes?'

John sat quietly for a while, trying to think of a way to explain it to them. At last he spoke.

'Jesus once came across a man who had been blind since birth. He made a paste with some mud, and spread it on the man's eyes. Then Jesus told him to go and wash in the pool of Siloam. When the man obeyed, he found he could see. The people brought him to the Pharisees, who wanted to know how he had been cured. He told them what Jesus had done, but they wouldn't believe him.

'The Pharisees sent for the man's parents, to check that he really had been blind from birth. When they found that this was so, they asked him again to tell them exactly what Jesus had done.

'"I told you before, but you wouldn't listen," he said to them. "Do you want me to tell you it all again? Do you want to become his disciples?"

'This made the Pharisees very angry. "You may be one of his disciples, but we are disciples of Moses," they said. "We know that God spoke to Moses, but we don't know where Jesus gets his authority."

'The man who had been born blind laughed scornfully. "Well, that's an extraordinary thing," he said. "This man cured my blindness, and you don't know where his power comes from! If Jesus was not sent from God, he couldn't have done anything."

'"Who are you, to give us lessons in theology?" the

Pharisees said angrily. And they expelled him from the synagogue.

'When Jesus heard what they had done, he went to look for the man he had cured. "Don't worry about the Pharisees," he said. "Do you believe in the Son of Man?"

'"Tell me who the Son of Man is, sir, and I'll tell you whether I believe in him," the man replied.

'"It is he who is speaking to you now," Jesus said.

'"Sir, I do have faith in you," the man replied.

'"This is the reason I came into the world," Jesus said to the people around. "I have come to bring judgement. Some people respond to my light, they believe in it, and they learn to see. Others turn away from the light, and become blind."

'Some of the Pharisees realised that Jesus meant they were blind – inwardly blind. Perhaps that will help you to understand what Paul meant by inward eyes.'

John often spoke of the new quality of life Jesus had brought. He called it 'eternal life', and this used to confuse some of his hearers at Ephesus.

'Do you mean we shall live for ever?' they asked.

John thought for a moment.

'Jesus had some friends who lived in the village of Bethany, near Jerusalem,' he said. 'There were two sisters, called Martha and Mary, and their brother Lazarus. One day Lazarus became seriously ill, and his sisters sent for Jesus in the hope that he could cure him. But by the time Jesus arrived, Lazarus had been dead for four days, and was already laid in a tomb.

'Martha went out to meet Jesus. "Master, if only you had been here, my brother would not have died," she said.

'"Don't be afraid," Jesus said to her. "Your brother will live again."

'Martha hardly dared to hope. "I know he will rise again at the last day," she whispered.

'"I am the resurrection, and I am life," Jesus said. "Anyone who has faith in me, even if he dies, will live again. Do you believe this?"

'"Master, I do," Martha replied. "I know now that you are the Messiah."

'Martha went to fetch her sister Mary, and together they took Jesus to the tomb where Lazarus had been buried. It was a cave, with a great stone across the entrance.

'"Roll away the stone," Jesus commanded. They looked at him aghast.

'"But, master, it has been four days!" Martha said. "Surely ... his body ... will have begun to ..." She couldn't bring herself to finish the sentence.

'"If you have faith, you will see the glory of God," Jesus said firmly. They rolled back the stone.

'"Father, I thank you," Jesus prayed. Then he faced the mouth of the cave.

'"Lazarus, come out!" he called. To the astonishment and terror of all who were watching, Lazarus walked out of the cave, still wrapped in the grave clothes.

'"Free him of his wrappings, and let him go," Jesus commanded.

John paused, and looked at his hearers, who were waiting open-mouthed.

'That is another clue for you,' he said. 'You must think it out for yourselves.'

One thing in the gospels the early Christians used to keep coming back to time after time was the question of Jesus's suffering. They knew that the gospel writers linked the mission of Jesus with the suffering servant in Isaiah, but they couldn't understand why he had to be a servant. Surely the Messiah meant king, not servant? John remembered an incident towards the end of the ministry of Jesus which he thought would show them what kind of Messiah Jesus was.

'When we had our last meal with Jesus,' he said, 'the night that he was betrayed, he took a towel and wrapped it round his waist, and filled a basin with water. Then he began to wash our feet, and dry them with the towel. Peter wouldn't let him at first; he said it wasn't right. But Jesus insisted on doing it.

'Afterwards, Jesus asked us if we understood what he had done for us.

'"You call me Master and Lord," he said. "And rightly so, for that is what I am. Now if I, your master, have washed your feet, you ought also to be prepared to wash one another's feet. Don't expect to lord it over other people; you are called to follow my example, and serve others."

'That was just before Judas went out and betrayed him.'

John fell silent, lost in the memories of that awful night.

'John, I know you always tell us we should have faith,' one of his friends said. 'But I often find myself doubting some of these things I read in the gospels.'

John roused himself, and smiled.

'You mustn't worry about that,' he said. 'Have I never told you about Thomas?'

They shook their heads.

'It was on that first Sunday, after the Friday Jesus was crucified,' John began. 'We were indoors, absolutely terrified, thinking everything was lost, when suddenly Jesus appeared to us. We were transformed; everything was suddenly all right again. Now Thomas, one of the twelve, wasn't with the rest of us when Jesus appeared. We told him about it, of course, but he wouldn't believe us.

'"Unless I see the nail marks in his wrists, and see the wound in his side, and actually touch him, I won't believe it," he said.

'Well, a week later, Jesus appeared to us again, and this time Thomas was with us. To be honest, Thomas was afraid Jesus would be angry with him for not believing. But Jesus smiled at Thomas, and invited him to touch the nail marks in his wrist and the wound in his side. Thomas was deeply ashamed, and

said to Jesus, "My Lord and my God."

'It's not surprising that you have doubts, if even a disciple like Thomas could not believe without seeing. Pray, and faith will come.'

13 The Early Church

The book of the Acts of the Apostles is a continuation of the gospel of Luke. It is not a history of the early Church, nor is it a biography of Paul. The author was in all probability the doctor, Luke, referred to by Paul in his letter to the Colossians, in chapter 4, verse 14. His purpose is to show that God's messianic promises were fulfilled in Jesus, and that through the saving work of Jesus, Israel was reconstituted. Although continuous with the old Israel, after Jesus it extended to all who had faith in him, even non-Jews.

ACTS OF THE APOSTLES 2-8   JOEL 2   ISAIAH 53

The disciples were meeting together to celebrate the Feast of Weeks, the Jewish harvest festival. This was also known as Pentecost, because it took place fifty days after the Passover. They were happy and confident again when they knew Jesus was alive, and Peter was emerging as their natural leader. But so far they had not said anything to anybody outside their own group.

While they were sitting at table, there was suddenly a sound like a gale-force wind through the whole house. As they looked at each other, they saw that every one of them was somehow transformed. When they tried to describe the experience afterwards, they said it looked as if flames of fire were resting on them. It was a tremendous religious experience for all of them. They knew, suddenly, that the Spirit of God which Jesus had promised had come to them. Full of confidence, they went out and began to preach the good news of Jesus Christ to all the

pilgrims who were then in Jerusalem.

The sight of the disciples, excited and talkative, rushing out on to the streets and telling every stranger they met about Jesus, amazed the people of Jerusalem. Some said openly that they must be drunk. On one such occasion, Peter stood up in the square and spoke to the crowd.

'I know what you are saying about us, my friends,' he said. 'But I assure you we are not drunk. What you are seeing today is a fulfilment of the prophet Joel:

The day will come, says your Lord God,
When I will pour out my spirit on all mankind.
Your sons and daughters shall prophesy,
Old men see dreams, and young men visions,
Even slaves will receive my spirit.
There will be signs in the sky, and on the earth;
Blood and fire and clouds of smoke.
The sun will go dark, and the moon turn to blood,
Before the great and terrible day of the Lord.
Only those who call on the Lord by name will be
    saved.

'My friends, I am speaking to you today about the

man Jesus of Nazareth, well known to you all because of his teaching and the marvellous works which God performed through him. You had him crucified, but God raised him to life again, as we can all bear witness. All that you are seeing and hearing now comes from him.'

Many of the Jewish people listening to Peter's speech were deeply impressed, and asked Peter what they should do. Peter told them to repent and be baptised, and many people became Christians that day.

From then on, Peter, John and the disciples preached openly about Jesus, and those who believed and followed gave up everything they had and lived in one big community. Peter and John were arrested several times, but they had such a following among the people that the authorities had to let them go. One of the Pharisees, a man called Gamaliel, pointed out that there had been several false messiahs before Jesus.

'If this Jesus movement is not from God, it will soon collapse,' he said. 'But if it is from God, we should not oppose it. I suggest we leave it alone, and see what happens.'

The Jewish council took his advice, and Peter and John and the other apostles were able to continue preaching to the people. By now, there were so many believers that the organisation of the community became very complex. The twelve called the whole group together, and suggested that they elect seven men from among their number, to act as organisers. This was done, and the organisers became known as deacons. The apostles laid their hands on the deacons as a sign that they were ordained by God for a special purpose.

One of the seven deacons was a man called Stephen, and he soon began to prove his worth to the movement. He was a marvellous preacher, and he commanded attention wherever he went. Many people were converted to the faith by hearing Stephen or seeing him heal people. One group of Jews to whom Stephen had been sent to preach, however, were bitterly opposed to him. They argued with him, but when that did no good, they reported him to the authorities on false charges of blasphemy against Moses and God.

Stephen was brought before the Jewish council in Jerusalem to answer the charges. He saw this as a wonderful opportunity to preach to a wider audience, and proceeded to go through the entire history of the Jewish nation from Abraham onwards to show them how everything pointed to and led up to Jesus. They heard him out in silence until he told them that they and their forefathers had always killed the prophets who had foretold the coming of Jesus, and now they were guilty of murdering the Messiah himself.

At this the Jewish leaders became very angry, and began to threaten Stephen. But he wouldn't stop.

'I tell you, I can see Jesus whom you crucified!' he

cried. 'He stands at the right hand of God!'

This was too much for the council. They rushed forward, dragged Stephen outside and stoned him to death. Even as he was dying, Stephen prayed, 'Lord, do not hold this sin against them.' One of the Jews who watched Stephen die was a man from Tarsus named Saul, who was violently opposed to the Christians.

This marked a turning-point for the early Church. Until then, they had enjoyed much success in Jerusalem, and apart from occasional arrests, they had been left alone by the Jewish authorities. After Stephen's death, a period of terror began, led by Saul. Many Christians were thrown into prison, and others fled to remote country districts, where they continued to preach the word of God.

Philip, one of the seven deacons, found himself in the city of Gitta in Samaria, where he began preaching. This was the first time that the gospel had been proclaimed to non-Jews, and the people listened eagerly to Philip's message. Many were cured by Philip in the name of Jesus Christ, and many more were baptised.

When news reached the twelve in Jerusalem that Philip was winning converts in Samaria, they sent Peter and John to investigate. After all, the Samaritans were old enemies of the Jews; was it right to allow them to become Christians? When Peter and John arrived in Samaria, however, they were very impressed by the sincerity of Philip's converts. Peter and John laid their hands on the Samaritan Christians, and they were filled with the Spirit of God as the disciples had been at Pentecost.

Philip went back to Jerusalem with Peter and John. He felt that God had more work for him to do, and he carried on southwards on the desert road from Jerusalem to Gaza. On the way, he came across an important-looking official sitting in his carriage reading. Philip felt drawn to him, and went up to the carriage.

He saw that the man was a foreigner; he was, in fact, the chief treasurer of the queen of Ethiopia. Then Philip noticed that the book the man was reading was the scroll of the prophet Isaiah.

'Do you understand what you are reading?' Philip asked.

The Ethiopian looked up. 'I see you are Jewish,' he said. 'I would be most grateful if you would explain this passage to me.'

He invited Philip to sit in the carriage with him, and showed him the chapter he was finding difficult:

He was taken like a sheep to be slaughtered,
And like a lamb being sheared, he was silent.
He had no defence, and there was no justice;
He was led away to be killed,
And is cut off from the world of the living.

The official put down the scroll, and asked Philip whether the prophet had been writing about

himself or someone else.

Philip took a deep breath, and starting with the prophets, began to explain to the Ethiopian the good news about Jesus. His hearer was deeply moved, and believed at once. They came to a river, and he ordered the carriage to be stopped.

'Here is some water,' he said to Philip. 'What is there to stop me being baptised now?' They got out of the carriage, and Philip baptised him in the river.

14 Paul and the Mission to the Gentiles

Paul-Saul, who was first called Saul and later Paul, in fact had both names from birth. He was an Aramaic-speaking Jew, but was born in Tarsus in Cilicia. His father, although Jewish, was a Roman citizen. Paul-Saul studied in Jerusalem under Gamaliel, possibly with the intention of becoming a rabbi. His conversion on the road to Damascus was from Judaism to Christ. He understood his experience as an act of God's grace; Jesus had appeared to him, Saul, the persecutor of the Church. This experience laid the foundation for much of Paul's later theology.

In the account of the first missionary journey by Barnabas and Saul, the pattern of Luke's two-volume book is repeated: rejection by the Jews, and acceptance by the Gentiles. The John-Mark who accompanied Barnabas and Saul may have been the author of the gospel of Mark.

ACTS OF THE APOSTLES 9-11,13,14

Saul decided it was time the followers of Jesus were stopped for good. He heard that they were particularly strong in Damascus, so he obtained letters from the high priest giving him authority to arrest anyone he found there following the new way, and to bring them to Jerusalem for trial.

While he was on the road to Damascus, a blinding light suddenly surrounded Saul. He fell to the ground, covering his eyes, and heard a voice speaking to him:

'Saul, Saul, why are you trying to destroy me?'

'Who are you?' Saul asked, trembling.

'I am Jesus. When you attack my followers, you are attacking me. Get up and go on into Damascus, and you will find out what you must do.'

Saul's companions stood around him, not sure what to do. They could hear him speaking, but they couldn't see anyone. They thought he was having some kind of fit.

'Saul, are you all right?' they said, helping him to his feet.

'Take me into Damascus,' Saul replied, holding out his hands. His friends saw that he was blind, and led him carefully into the city. He was blind for three days, and would not eat or drink.

One of the disciples in Damascus was a man called Ananias. He had a dream in which God told him to go to the house where Saul was staying, and give him back his sight. When he woke up, Ananias was reluctant to go; he knew Saul's reputation, and he was afraid. But the dream stayed with him, clear and sharp, and he knew he must obey.

When Ananias came to the house, he found Saul kneeling in prayer.

'Saul, my brother,' Ananias said to him softly. Saul

turned his head, and Ananias saw that he was indeed blind.

'Who is it?' Saul asked.

'My name is Ananias. I have been sent by the Lord Jesus, who appeared to you while you were on your way to Damascus.'

Ananias went over to Saul, placed his hands on Saul's head, and prayed. Suddenly, Saul found that he could see again. From that day on, he was a changed man. He was baptised in the name of Jesus, and instead of arresting the disciples in Damascus, he became one of them. They were suspicious of him at first, because of what he had done against the disciples in Jerusalem, but when he began to preach about Jesus openly in the synagogues in Damascus, they knew he was genuine, and accepted him.

The people who heard Saul preach were amazed.

'Can this really be Saul, who came here to arrest the followers of Jesus?' they said. But Saul was growing more and more confident, and was soon as forceful and persuasive in his arguments for Jesus as he had previously been in his opposition to him. The Jews in Damascus who didn't follow Jesus decided to kill him, but the disciples heard of the plot in time and

helped Saul to escape. They lowered him over the city wall in a basket during the night, and Saul made his way back to Jerusalem.

The disciples in Jerusalem were very surprised when Saul told them he wanted to join them. At first they wouldn't have anything to do with him in case it was a trap, but Barnabas told them that Jesus had appeared to Saul on the road to Damascus, and they realised that he was a changed man. Soon Saul was preaching openly and fearlessly in Jerusalem just as Stephen had done.

The Jewish leaders were very put out. Saul had been well known for his opposition to the disciples. After he had changed sides, he won many converts to Jesus Christ. The Jews decided there was only one thing for it – he would have to be killed. Just in time, the disciples heard of their plans, and hurriedly took Saul to Caesarea, where he took a ship to Tarsus.

Peter visited the disciples in various towns in Judaea, and stayed for a while in the coastal town of Joppa where he brought back to life a woman who had died, called Dorcas. Peter was worried about the way that Christianity was spreading, particularly since Philip had baptised the Ethiopian. Was it right to admit non-Jews to the brotherhood? He went up to the roof of the house where he was staying, to think and pray. It was a long time since he had eaten, and he began to feel faint. He was looking out across the harbour at a sailing boat, its great sail billowing in the wind, when he fell into a trance. It seemed to him that the sail came nearer and nearer, until it was spread out on the rooftop at his feet. When he looked down, Peter saw that the sail was full of animals and birds that Jews were not supposed to eat – pigs, camels, hares, vultures, crows and owls. Then, in his trance, Peter heard a voice.

'If you are hungry, Peter, kill and eat.' Peter was disgusted.

'I have never eaten anything unclean,' he protested.

'Who are you to say what is clean and what is unclean?' the voice replied. Slowly Peter came out of the trance, and began to wonder what it had meant.

Just then, messengers arrived at the house asking for Peter. He went downstairs to see what they wanted.

'We have been sent by Cornelius, a centurion in Caesar's army, based at Caesarea,' they replied. 'He is a devout and God-fearing man, as your friends will tell you, even though he is not a Jew. Cornelius has had a message from God telling him to invite you to his house.'

Peter asked the messenger in, and next day he and some of his friends went with them to Caesarea.

When they arrived, Cornelius came out and bowed low at Peter's feet.

'Stand up, there's a good fellow,' said Peter, embarrassed. 'No need for that, I'm only a man, remember. Now, what is all this about?'

Cornelius told him about the message he had had from God.

'And now you are here, and we are ready to listen to what you have to say,' he concluded.

Suddenly Peter understood the meaning of the vision he had had on the rooftop at Joppa. God had been showing him that the good news of Jesus Christ was for all men – not just for the Jews. He told Cornelius all about Jesus, and then baptised him and all his family in the name of Jesus Christ.

When Peter got back to Jerusalem, he had to explain to the Church there what he had done. When he told them about his vision at Joppa, they accepted that it was God's will that the good news should be proclaimed to all the nations of the world. Before long, Gentiles (that is, non-Jews) were joining the church everywhere, without having to become Jews first. One of the centres where this began to happen was Antioch, in Syria, where there were many followers of Jesus. Barnabas was sent from Jerusalem to check on what was happening at Antioch. He found that they were all genuine converts, and sent back good reports to Jerusalem. He also sent for his friend Saul, who left Tarsus and joined him in

Antioch, where they stayed for some time. It was in Antioch that the disciples first became known as Christians.

The Church in Antioch decided that it was God's will that Barnabas and Saul should be sent out to preach the gospel of Jesus in other countries. Taking John-Mark with them, these two went to the Syrian port of Seleucia, and took a boat to the island of Cyprus, which was the homeland of Barnabas. They arrived at the port of Salamis, and travelled the length of the island, preaching the word of God in all the Jewish synagogues.

They came to Paphos, at the western end of the island of Cyprus, where there lived a Jewish magician called Elymas, who had a great deal of influence over the governor, Sergius Paulus. Elymas saw Barnabas and Saul as rivals, and tried to persuade the governor not to listen to them. Saul, who by this time was beginning to be known by his second name of Paul, confronted Elymas.

'You double-dealing, lying trickster!' he said. 'How dare you interfere with the work of the Lord? You shall be struck blind for a time, so that you may know just how powerful the Lord really is!'

At these words, Elymas lost the power of sight, and groped about for someone to lead him by the hand. The governor was most impressed, and was converted to Christianity by Paul.

Leaving Cyprus, Barnabas and Paul went by boat northwards to the region of Pamphylia, present-day Turkey. John-Mark, however, returned to Jerusalem. Barnabas and Paul visited several towns, preaching first of all in the Jewish synagogues, and only when they were rejected by the Jews, turning to the Gentiles.

In one town, Lystra, there was a crippled man whom Paul cured. The townsfolk were terrified at this display of power, and thought that Barnabas and Paul must be gods walking on earth. The rumour quickly went round that Barnabas was Jupiter, their chief god, and Paul was Mercury, the messenger of the gods, because he was the spokesman. Barnabas and Paul only just managed to prevent the crowds from sacrificing oxen to them at the temple of Jupiter.

Then some Jews arrived from the other towns Barnabas and Paul had visited, and turned the crowd against them. Angry at being deceived by Barnabas and Paul, as they thought, the people of Lystra began to stone them, and they barely escaped with their lives. They retraced their footsteps, strengthening and encouraging the converts they had made, and appointing elders in each of the newly-formed churches. Then they sailed back to Antioch, to report on the success of the first mission to the Gentiles.

15 Paul's Second Missionary Journey

*Acts chapter 15 refers again to the question
of admitting non-Jews to the Christian
brotherhood. The chapter raises a number
of difficulties. The matter had apparently
already been settled in chapter 11, after
the Cornelius episode. Paul nowhere
mentions the decision of the Council in his
letters, and Luke's accounts of Paul's visits
to Jerusalem are impossible to harmonise
with Paul's own account in Galatians
chapters 1 and 2. For these reasons, Acts
chapter 15 is omitted here.*

*The Silas who accompanied Paul on his
second journey is probably the Sylvanus
referred to in several of Paul's epistles.
The narrative in Acts switches to first
person plural on the journey to Philippi,
possibly indicating that Luke joined the
party; to avoid confusion, this change is
not used here.*

ACTS OF THE APOSTLES 16–18
PHILIPPIANS 2   I THESSALONIANS 4
I CORINTHIANS 13

After they had been back in Antioch for some time,
Paul suggested to Barnabas that they ought to revisit
the churches they had founded on their first journey.
Barnabas agreed, but wanted to take John-Mark with
them again. Paul didn't want him, because John-
Mark had left them in Cyprus. This led to a bitter
argument, and eventually Paul and Barnabas split
up; Barnabas took Mark and went to Cyprus, while
Paul went to Turkey accompanied by Silas. Paul and
Silas revisited all the churches there, and carried on

westwards until they came to the Aegean Sea at the port of Troas. They had not found any openings for preaching, and were feeling frustrated and unsure of themselves.

That night, Paul had a dream in which a man from the province of Macedonia, the European side of the Aegean Sea, appeared to him.

'Come over to Macedonia, Paul. We need you here,' the man said.

Next morning, Paul told Silas his dream, and they took the next available boat across the narrow sea to Macedonia, arriving eventually at the Roman colony of Philippi. Here they began to speak about Jesus Christ to people they met, starting with a group of Jews who met outside the city for worship on the sabbath.

One of the people they spoke to was a woman from the province of Lydia, who heard them gladly and believed at once. She and all her household were baptised, and she invited Paul and Silas back to her house. The woman and her family were the first European converts to Christianity.

While they were in Philippi, Paul and Silas were

followed about by a slave-girl who had what we would call today psychic powers. She was a fortune-teller, and used to earn a lot of money for her masters. She knew that Paul and Silas really were inspired by God, and she followed them wherever they went, shouting, 'These men are servants of God! They will save your souls!'

At last Paul, never the most patient of men, could stand it no longer. He rounded angrily on the girl.

'For goodness' sake, stop it!' he snapped. 'In the name of Jesus Christ, I order you to be quiet!'

The girl fell silent, and lost her powers of fortune-telling from then on. She felt much happier to be a normal person, but her owners were not so pleased; their source of profit had gone. They grabbed Paul and Silas and hauled them before the city magistrates.

'These fellows are stirring up trouble,' they alleged. 'They are Jews, and they are trying to get people to follow some new way which is illegal for Roman citizens.'

Paul and Silas protested their innocence, but the crowd supported the girl's owners, and the magistrates found Paul and Silas guilty. They were flogged, and thrown into prison.

At midnight that night, Paul and Silas were still awake, praying and singing hymns of praise to God to keep their spirits up. Suddenly there was a violent earthquake which shook the jail to its foundations. Doors burst open, walls crashed down, and Paul and Silas, who had been in chains, found themselves free.

In the silence that followed the earthquake, the jailer came running into the cells.

'Oh no! All the doors open!' he wailed. 'The prisoners will all have escaped, and I'll be blamed!' He drew his sword, ready to commit suicide.

'Put down your sword!' Paul called to him. 'We are all still here!'

The jailer called for lights, and came up to Paul, trembling with fear.

'Now I really believe in your God,' he said. 'What do I have to do, to save my life?'

Paul and Silas told him all about the Lord Jesus, and the jailer and all his family believed and were baptised. He took the two apostles back to his own house, bathed their wounds and gave them a meal.

Next morning, the city magistrates sent word to the jailer that Paul and Silas were to be released. The jailer came and told Paul.

'Oh yes?' said Paul scornfully. 'They flog us and throw us into prison, when we've done nothing wrong, and now they want us to leave quietly out of the back door? Not likely! I'm a Roman citizen, and I know my rights – I demand a public apology!'

When the magistrates heard that Paul was a Roman citizen, they were very worried and came down in person to offer their apologies. Paul agreed to leave the city, after first going to say goodbye to his fellow-Christians.

The Christians in Philippi never found things easy. Some years later, when they were being persecuted for their beliefs, Paul wrote to encourage them. Paul was in prison himself at the time, either in Ephesus or Rome, and he wrote to the Philippians as fellow-sufferers. He urged them to try and be like Jesus: 'Jesus was with God from the first; yet he did not try to rule over others like a god, but made himself a mere slave. He accepted all the limitations of being human, even death on a cross. So you, my brothers, must be obedient to God, wherever it leads you.'

On leaving Philippi, Paul and Silas went further west to Thessalonica, where the Jewish community listened to Paul and some were converted. Others, however, stirred up a riot against them, and Paul and Silas had to leave hurriedly for Beroea. The Jews in Beroea were much more welcoming; they listened eagerly to what Paul had to say, and many Jews as well as some Gentiles in Beroea became believers. The Thessalonian Jews, however, heard how well Paul was doing in Beroea, and came down to stir up a mob against him. Again, Paul had to leave hurriedly for his own safety. Silas stayed behind, with Timothy, another companion, to carry on Paul's work.

This time, Paul went south into Greece, to the city of Athens. Here he preached to the Jewish community in their synagogue, and also to the Greeks in the market-place. His preaching aroused considerable interest among the Athenians, who loved to argue and discuss different philosophies. They invited him to give a lecture at the ancient Greek court of Areopagus, which was held just outside Athens at a place called Mars' Hill. (Mars was one of their gods.)

'Men of Athens,' Paul began. 'I can see that in matters of religion, you are very cautious. On my way here today, I noticed an altar labelled, "To An Unknown God". I am here today to tell you about that God you worship but do not know.'

He went on to tell them all about God and Jesus, ending with Jesus's death and resurrection. At this, some of the Greeks scoffed openly, and others thanked him politely and said they would like to hear him again sometime. Paul realised that they were only interested in arguing. He left Athens in despair, and went on to Corinth.

Here Paul was rejoined by Silas and Timothy, who brought good news of the young church in Thessalonica. Paul wrote warmly to the Thessalonians, encouraging them in the Christian life and reminding them of his earlier visit there. At that time, Paul firmly believed and had taught the Thessalonians that Jesus would soon be coming back to earth. He heard from Silas that some of them were worried about what would happen to Christians who died before Jesus came back, and he wrote to reassure them: 'We believe that Jesus died and rose again, and it will be the same for those who die as Christians; God will give them new life in Jesus. When the Lord comes again, the Christians who have died will be raised from the dead, and the Christians who are alive will join them and be taken up to heaven.'

Paul stayed in Corinth for some eighteen months, supporting himself by working at his old trade, that of a tent-maker. At first, he concentrated on preaching to the Jews in the synagogue, but when they turned against him, Paul again began to preach to the Gentiles and won many converts.

The Jews were very annoyed about Paul's success, and dragged him before the Roman governor, Gallio,

on false charges of persuading the people to follow an illegal religion. Gallio, although he had only recently taken over as governor in the region, was not easily deceived.

'If this had been a criminal matter, I would of course have given you a fair hearing,' he said. 'But this is just a squabble about Jewish laws; you can sort it out for yourselves.' And he had them thrown out of the court. Even when a mob of Greeks set upon the leaders of the Jewish synagogue and beat them up, Gallio would not interfere.

Paul eventually left Corinth and returned by sea to Antioch in Syria. The Christian church in Corinth had many problems, and Paul later wrote to them several times to try and sort out their difficulties. One of the most famous passages Paul wrote was in a letter to the Corinthians, when he was trying to explain to them the true meaning of the word 'love':

Now I will show you the best way to live. I may speak like an angel, but if I have no love, I will sound like the clatter of a dustbin lid.

I may have the gift of second sight, and be able to foretell the future; but without love, I am useless.

Love is patient; love is kind, and doesn't envy anyone. Love is not boastful or rude, nor is it easily offended. Love does not nurse grievances or gloat over other people's misfortunes. There is nothing love cannot face up to.

Prophecies, visions, knowledge – all these are partial, and will fade away. There are three things that will last for ever – faith, hope and love. But of these, the greatest is love.

16 Paul Revisits Asia

*Paul's third journey began almost
immediately after his return to Antioch.
He revisited the churches in Galatia and
Phrygia and made his way to Ephesus.
The presence in Ephesus of Christians
who had received only 'John's baptism'
indicates something of the variety of
experience of the early Church. The success
of Paul's mission in Ephesus led to
opposition, not from the Jews, but from
the worshippers of the Greek goddess Artemis,
or Diana, the goddess of fertility. The
symbol of Diana which 'fell from heaven'
was most probably a meteorite. Luke makes
no mention of other troubles at Ephesus
referred to by Paul in his letters to the
Corinthians.*

*Paul went to Corinth again to strengthen
the churches in Macedonia, and it was
probably during this time that the epistle
to the Romans was written.*

ACTS OF THE APOSTLES 18-20   ROMANS 5

Paul spent some time in Antioch among his friends,
resting and recovering his strength. He soon began to
feel restless, however, and decided it was time to
revisit the churches in Turkey where he had made so
many converts. He travelled through the whole
region, encouraging and strengthening the believers,
until he came to Ephesus on the west coast. Here, to
his surprise, he found a group of people who called
themselves Christians. Paul was very pleased to find a
church in Ephesus, but he was a bit puzzled by some
of their beliefs.

'Have you been baptised?' he asked them.

Ephesus

'Oh, yes,' they told him proudly. 'We've all received the baptism that John the Baptist gave his followers. We're waiting for the Messiah to come – the Christ that John the Baptist said would come after him.'

Patiently, Paul explained to them about the life and death of Jesus, who was the Christ that John the Baptist had prophesied. He told them that Jesus still lived, and that his Holy Spirit helped and supported all who believed in him. They believed at once, and were baptised by Paul in the name of Jesus.

Paul stayed on in Ephesus, spending three months trying to convert the Jewish people in the synagogue there. When at last he could make no headway with them, he turned again to the non-Jews, making many converts.

Ephesus was a centre for the worship of the goddess Diana. There was a temple dedicated to Diana, and her symbol was a great stone which was said to have fallen from the sky. People came from all over the province to worship Diana, and the local silversmiths used to make little silver statues of the goddess which they sold to the pilgrims. One of the leaders of the silversmiths was a man called Demetrius. He was very concerned about the way the trade in silver statues was falling off as a result of Paul's efforts. He called a meeting of the local silversmiths and other tradesmen, and stood up to speak to them.

'Fellow workers!' he began. 'You all know how we rely on making and selling statues of Diana for our living. This fellow Paul is turning people away from Diana and converting them to a new religion which doesn't allow statues or idols. He has already won many followers here in Ephesus, and I'm told in many other towns as well. I'm not just thinking of our trade, you realise; I'm thinking of the honour of our goddess Diana. If this carries on, Diana will be forgotten completely!'

At this, the tradesmen were carried away and began shouting angrily and banging the tables.

'Diana is the greatest!' shouted one voice, loud and clear. This was taken up by the others, and the whole mob surged out on to the streets, chanting 'Diana is the greatest!' as loudly as they could. They seized hold of two of Paul's friends, and dragged them off to the theatre in the middle of the town. As soon as Paul heard what had happened, he wanted to go to the theatre and speak to the crowd, but the other Christians would not let him.

Meanwhile, in the theatre, things were in a state of confusion. Some of the crowd were shouting one thing, some another. Fights were breaking out, and it began to look very serious for the Christians. Some of the Jews in the crowd were afraid that they would be attacked, as well as the Christians. They pushed their spokesman, Alexander, to the front to explain that they were not Christians, and that Paul's activities had nothing to do with them. But when the crowd realised he was a Jew, they wouldn't even let him speak. The chanting began again: 'Diana is the greatest!'

This went on for nearly two hours. At last the town clerk managed to quieten them down.

'Men of Ephesus!' he said to them. 'I know how concerned you are, but if you have a case against Paul and his followers, you must take it to the law-courts in the proper way. Remember we are part of the Roman empire. Do you want to be charged with rioting? This behaviour is unforgiveable. Take yourselves off home at once, and let's do things through the proper channels.'

After it had quietened down, Paul stayed to make sure that the Christians in Ephesus were all right, and then set off for Macedonia and Greece. It was during this time that Paul wrote one of his most important letters, to the Christians in Rome. Many of the early Christians were Jews, and they found it difficult to accept non-Jews who did not follow the law of Moses. Paul wanted to explain to them that the good news of Jesus was the fulfilment of the law of Moses, and that it was God's will that the Jews should accept Jesus as their Messiah and make him known to the rest of the world.

Macedonia

'It's no good saying that you obey the law of Moses,' Paul wrote. 'That won't justify you in the eyes of God. We're none of us good enough on our own to be acceptable to God. You have to have faith in God, and trust him completely. It's only through the kindness of his heart that we are forgiven.

'Let me put it this way. Sin came into the world through one man, Adam. The result of his act of disobedience was that from then on, all men were condemned to die. By the grace of God, one man, Jesus Christ, died for us, and freed us from the sentence of death. Jesus was a second Adam, coming to our rescue.'

Paul stayed in Greece for some months, eventually making his way back through Macedonia and across to the port of Troas in Asia Minor. Here the Christians assembled as usual for the breaking of bread on the Saturday night, and Paul gave a talk. They were meeting in an upstairs room; it was very hot and stuffy, and the oil lamps were making the room smoky. One young man, whose name was Eutychus, was sitting on a window sill. As Paul's talk went on and on, Eutychus felt himself getting sleepy.

Finally he dozed off, and fell backwards through the open window, landing with a dreadful crash on the ground below.

The service was halted immediately while the Christians hurried downstairs to see what had happened. Eutychus lay sprawled on the ground, unconscious and scarcely breathing; indeed, the first ones on the scene took him for dead and began to cry and wail.

Paul pushed his way through and took Eutychus in his arms.

'Stop that noise!' he commanded. 'He's still alive.'

He began to pray aloud to God, and the other Christians fell to their knees and joined him. Eutychus began to stir, his eyes opened, and he recovered. To the Christians in Troas, it was a miracle, just like Elijah and the widow's son, or Peter and Dorcas.

Paul and his companions left Troas and made their way by sea to Jerusalem, as Paul was anxious to be there in time for the festival of Pentecost.

17 Paul Returns to Jerusalem

Despite warnings from his friends, Paul was determined to go to Jerusalem. Agabus seems to have been a prophet in the Old Testament tradition. He used symbolic prophecy, rather like Isaiah (Isaiah chapter 20) and Jeremiah (Jeremiah chapter 13) to show God's intentions. The prophet's action was thought to bring about that which it symbolised.

In Jerusalem, Paul was asked by James to undergo a period of ritual purification from the uncleanness caused by his time spent among Gentiles. This was intended to convince the zealous Jews that he still conformed to Jewish law.

The 'Jews from Asia' were Jews of the Dispersion, who were very strict about observance of the law which distinguished them from their pagan neighbours. The essence of Paul's defence, however, was that he was a devout Jew and that the mission to the Gentiles was a fulfilment of the Jewish law.

ACTS OF THE APOSTLES 21-23

When Paul and his travelling companions returned from Paul's third missionary journey, they arrived back at the northern port of Ptolemais and stayed with the Christians there for a while. Paul was determined to press on to Jerusalem, despite the fact that opposition to the Christian movement was strongest there.

While they were in Ptolemais, a prophet from Judaea whose name was Agabus came to see them. He was a dramatic figure, dressed in camelskin and carrying a staff, just like one of the prophets of old. He came striding into the house, demanding to see Paul.

He took Paul's leather belt, and bound his own hands and feet with it.

'This is what the Jews in Jerusalem will do to the man who owns this belt,' he declared. 'They will bind him hand and foot, and hand him over to the Gentiles.'

The Christians there were very distressed, and begged Paul in tears not to go to Jerusalem.

'Why are you crying?' Paul asked. 'You know my mind is made up. I am quite prepared, not merely to be tied hand and foot, but to die in Jerusalem for the Lord Jesus, if that is the will of God.'

His friends gave up trying to change Paul's mind, and helped him pack. He set off on the road to Jerusalem, accompanied by some Christians from Caesarea and a Jerusalem Christian called Mason, who was going to give him lodgings while he was in the capital.

On arrival in Jerusalem, Paul went to pay his respects to James the brother of Jesus, who had become the leader of the Church in Jerusalem. He told James about his work among the Gentiles, and the success they had had in Asia and Greece. James looked thoughtful.

'I am delighted that so many non-Jews have turned to Jesus,' he said. 'But it gives me something of a problem here in Jerusalem. You see, Paul, all the Christians here are Jews, and firm supporters of the law of Moses. They have heard rumours that you are teaching that that law is no longer important.'

'But surely they don't believe that!' Paul burst out angrily.

'Take it easy, Paul,' James replied. 'I don't believe it, because I know you better. What I suggest you do is this. There are four Jewish Christians here who have taken a vow as Nazirites. They are going to go through seven days of purification, following the Jewish law, ending by sacrificing publicly in the temple. I want you to go through the ritual with them. Then everyone will see that you are a loyal Jew as well as a Christian.'

Paul did as James suggested, and at the end of the seven-day period, went with the four men to offer sacrifices in the temple. Some Jews from Ephesus happened to be there when Paul came in, and they recognised him at once.

'It's that trouble-maker Paul!' they shouted. 'Paul the friend of Gentiles! Paul the law-breaker!'

A crowd began to form, and Paul was surrounded by angry, hostile faces.

'He defiled the temple!' someone shouted. 'He brought a Gentile in here!'

There was a roar of anger, and the crowd closed in menacingly.

'Kill him! Death to Paul!'

The mob surged in and swept Paul out of the temple into the public square, ready to lynch him.

Paul tried in vain to defend himself, but couldn't make himself heard against the uproar. Then there was the welcome sound of running feet and clanking armour, and a force of Roman soldiers appeared. They scattered the mob, picked Paul up and arrested him.

'Now then, what's going on?' demanded the centurion in charge. All the crowd began shouting at once, and the centurion couldn't make out what they were saying. He ordered his men to take Paul to the barracks, and they dragged him off with the crowd baying at his heels.

When they came to the gate of the Roman garrison, Paul managed to speak to the centurion.

'May I have a word with you?' he asked. He spoke in Greek, the common language of the Roman empire. The centurion was surprised to find he was an educated man.

'You speak Greek, do you? Then you're not that Egyptian rebel we've been looking for?' Apparently, there had been an attempted coup some days before, led by an Egyptian who had escaped.

'No, indeed,' Paul replied. 'I am a Jew, from the city of Tarsus. If you will permit me, I would like to speak to the people.'

The centurion agreed, and his men silenced the mob. Paul spoke to them in their own language, Aramaic, and they began to listen.

'I am a true-born Jew,' Paul began. 'I was brought up here in Jerusalem, and studied the law as a pupil of Gamaliel. Some of you may remember that when this Christian movement started, I was opposed to it and myself arrested many Christians.

'On my way to Damascus to round up more of the followers of Jesus, I had a complete change of heart. Jesus himself appeared to me in a vision, and ordered me to go and preach to the Gentiles.'

This was too much for the crowd. They began to howl for Paul's blood, and the centurion hurriedly ordered him to be brought into the barracks for his own safety.

'Tie the fellow up, and flog him,' he ordered. 'We'll find out then what this is all about.' He hadn't been able to follow Paul's speech, and couldn't understand why the crowd wanted to lynch him.

As the soldiers were tying Paul to the whipping-post, he called out to the centurion.

'Can you legally flog a Roman citizen, who has not been found guilty on any charge?'

The centurion came over to Paul at once.

'What do you mean?' he said. 'I thought you said you were a Jew?'

'I am a Roman citizen by birth,' Paul replied.

The centurion ordered his men to untie Paul at once, and hurried to report to the commandant. They detained Paul overnight, and next morning, the commandant called a meeting of the Jewish council to try and find out just what the charges were against Paul.

When the chief priests and Jewish elders were assembled, he ordered Paul to be brought before them.

'I've no idea what they have against me,' Paul declared. 'My conscience is clear.'

'How can you say that!' exclaimed Ananias, the high priest. He motioned one of his men forward, and the man struck Paul across the mouth.

'May God strike you, you hypocrite!' retorted Paul. 'You sit there accusing me of breaking the law, and then you flout the law yourself by having me struck!'

Some of the attendants began to remonstrate with

A Pharisees

Paul for speaking against the high priest.

'Oh, I beg your pardon,' said Paul, with heavy sarcasm. 'I had no idea that he was the high priest.'

Paul could see that some of the council were Pharisees, and some Sadducees. He knew that the Pharisees taught that there was life after death, but the Sadducees denied this. Paul turned to the commandant.

'I'll tell you what the real issue is here, sir,' he said. 'I am a Pharisee, born and bred; some of these people are after my blood because I teach that there is life after death.'

The council immediately began to argue among themselves, with some of the Pharisees supporting Paul, and the Sadducees violently opposing him. Seeing that they were about to come to blows, and fearing for Paul's safety, the commandant had his troops take Paul back to the garrison.

That night, a group of Jews who wanted to get rid of Paul took an oath not to eat or drink until they had killed him. They went to the chief priests with their plan.

'Arrange for Paul to be brought before the full

council for a further examination tomorrow morning,' they said. 'We'll ambush him on the way, and kill him.'

The chief priests and elders agreed to this, but Paul's nephew got to hear of the plot and hurried to the Roman garrison to tell Paul. Paul beckoned one of the centurions over.

'Could you take this young man to see the commandant?' he asked. 'He has something of vital importance to report.'

When the commandant heard about the plot, he made arrangements for Paul to be taken under heavy escort to Caesarea, the headquarters of the Roman governor Felix.

18   The Shipwreck

In Caesarea, Paul appeared before the
Roman governor Felix, who was not convinced
by the Jewish argument and adjourned the
case. Felix kept Paul in custody for two
years, during which time he had many
talks with him; partly in the hope of
receiving a bribe, and partly because he
was genuinely interested in what Paul had
to say.

Felix was replaced when his tour of duty
came to an end, and the new governor,
Festus, had Paul brought before him. He
asked Paul if he would be willing to go back
to Jerusalem to stand trial there. Paul,
knowing he would not get a fair trial in
Jerusalem, exercised his right as a Roman
citizen and appealed to Caesar. Festus had
no option but to arrange for Paul to be
taken to Rome.

ACTS OF THE APOSTLES 27,28

Paul, together with other prisoners being sent to
Rome, was put in the charge of a centurion named
Julius, who arranged for them to take passage in a
trading ship bound for the Asian ports. They called
first at Sidon, then crossed the Mediterranean Sea to
the north of the island of Cyprus, arriving at the port
of Myra, which was as far as the ship was going.

In Myra, Julius found an Alexandrian ship bound
for Italy, and put his prisoners on board. The winds
were against them, but they managed to get as far as
the island of Crete, where they hugged the coast and
dropped anchor in the south-facing bay called Fair
Havens. By now it was October, and the weather had
broken.

Paul, who had had plenty of experience of sailing the Mediterranean, advised them not to go on. But the captain felt that Fair Havens was too open and exposed to spend the winter, and decided to go on to the port of Phoenix, further west along the coast of Crete. Phoenix had a more sheltered harbour, and the captain intended to spend the winter months there.

At first, helped by a south wind, they made good progress along the coast of Crete. But suddenly the weather changed; a fierce north-eastern wind off the

Cretan mountains sprang up, and they were blown out to sea.

The wind was so strong that they could do nothing except sail before it. They had a brief respite when they ran under the lee of a small island off Crete called Canda, which gave them the opportunity to get the ship's boat under control and hauled aboard, and pass some ropes under the hull of the ship to strengthen it. Then they realised that they were drifting towards the sand bank of Syrtis, to the west of Crete. They had no choice but to lower the mainsail and run before the wind again.

The storm lasted for days, and after the third day the sailors began to throw some of the heavy gear overboard, as the ship was in danger of being swamped in the heavy seas. They had gone for a long time without food, and most of them were giving up hope of ever coming through alive. Paul stood up on deck, holding on to the mast, and spoke to the ship's company, shouting against the wind.

'You should have listened to me when we were in Crete, friends. Then you wouldn't be in this plight.' Paul could never resist the opportunity to show that he was right. 'But keep your courage up. I am convinced that it is God's will that I should appear before the emperor in Rome. We may lose the ship, but none of you will be harmed.'

That night, the sailors could hear breakers and knew they were getting near to rocks. They took a sounding, which showed twenty fathoms (36 metres). A few minutes later, they took another sounding, and found they were in only fifteen fathoms of water. By now, the crash of the waves on the rocks could be heard clearly. The crew quickly dropped four sea-anchors from the stern, in the hope of preventing the ship from running aground.

Dragging against the heavy anchors, the ship slowed down. They could all hear the noise of the waves breaking on the rocks, and they prayed for daylight. Some of the sailors panicked and lowered the ship's boat, thinking they would stand more of a chance in that. But Paul saw them and shouted to the centurion.

'Don't let the sailors get away, or we won't be able to control the ship!'

The soldiers who were on board to guard the prisoners cut the ropes, and let the boat drop away. The night wore on, and just before dawn, Paul spoke to the ship's crew again.

'You've had nothing to eat for days now,' he said to them. 'You're going to need all your strength if we're to survive. Eat the food we have left, I beg you. Remember, we are all going to live through this nightmare; God will protect us.'

With that, Paul broke bread and began to eat. The others followed suit, then set to work lightening the ship by dumping the cargo of corn overboard. When day broke, they could see that they were indeed quite close to land. There were rocks along the coast in both directions, but ahead of them they could see what looked like a sandy beach. They decided to try and run the ship aground on the beach. The sailors set the sail and slipped the anchors, and creaking and groaning, the battered ship and its weary crew began to make for the beach.

But their troubles were not yet over. The ship was suddenly caught in a cross-current, which swept it on to the rocks. There was a terrible, grinding crash as the bows caught fast. Waves were crashing down on the stern, and there was a dreadful tearing, rending noise as the hull began to break up.

Some of the soldiers wanted to execute the

prisoners in case they swam ashore and escaped, but the centurion was determined to get Paul safely to Rome, and stopped them. He ordered everyone who could swim to jump overboard and make for the beach, and made the rest grab planks, barrels or bits of wreckage and float ashore. Dazed and battered, the survivors staggered through the surf to the beach. As Paul had foretold, not one life was lost.

The island turned out to be Melita, now called Malta, and the people who lived there came hurrying out to help the shipwrecked men. It was cold and had started to rain, so they piled up driftwood and lit a great fire on the beach to dry the survivors out and keep them warm. Paul was just throwing an armful of sticks on the fire when a snake, sensing the heat, wriggled out of the sticks and fastened on Paul's hand.

The islanders, seeing the snake hanging from Paul's hand, were sure that he had been fatally bitten.

'It is the will of the gods,' they said. 'This man must be a murderer. He may have escaped from the sea, but the gods will not let him live.'

Paul, however, calmly shook the snake off into the fire, and showed no ill effects. The islanders watched him closely, expecting him to drop down dead at any minute, but when nothing happened they changed their minds and decided he must be a god.

The chief of the nearby village was a man named Publius. He made his unexpected visitors welcome, and provided them with food, clothes and accommodation. The chief's father was ill, suffering from a fever which no one could cure. Paul went to see the sick man, prayed, and laid his hands on him; and the man recovered.

After this many other sick people on the island

were brought to Paul, and were cured. Paul and his companions were treated as guests of honour, and stayed on the island for the rest of the winter.

When spring came and the weather improved, the centurion booked their passage on a ship which had spent the winter in Malta, and so in due course they sailed to Italy and came to Rome. Paul was allowed to lodge in a private house at his own expense, and he stayed there for two years under house arrest, preaching the kingdom of God and the good news of Jesus Christ to all who visited him.

More Beaver Books

We hope you have enjoyed this Beaver Book. Here are some of the other titles:

Stories from the Old Testament A Beaver original. From the story of the Creation to that of Jonah, these stirring tales are specially recounted for children by John Bailey. Illustrated in colour throughout

The Mother Goose Book Beautifully illustrated in delicate colours by Alice and Martin Provensen, this book of nursery rhymes is ideal for younger readers or for reading aloud

The Beaver Book of Sewing A Beaver original. From sewing on a button to making a dress from a paper pattern, here is everything you need to know about the subject. Written by Janet Barber and illustrated by Virginia Lister

These and many other Beavers are available from your local bookshop or newsagent, or can be ordered direct from: Hamlyn Paperback Cash Sales, PO Box 11, Falmouth, Cornwall TR 109EN. Send a cheque or postal order made payable to the Hamlyn Publishing Group, for the price of the book plus postage at the following rates:
UK: 40p for the first book, 18p for the second book, and 13p for each additional book ordered to a maximum charge of £1.49;
BFPO and Eire: 40p for the first book, 18p for the second book, plus 13p per copy for the next 7 books and thereafter 7p per book;
OVERSEAS: 60p for the first book and 18p for each extra book.

New Beavers are published every month and if you would like the *Beaver Bulletin*, a newsletter which tells you about new books and gives a complete list of titles and prices, send a large stamped addressed envelope to:

205088

Beaver Bulletin
The Hamlyn Group
Astronaut House
Feltham
Middlesex TW14 9AR